Professional Preparation for Teachers of Exceptional Children

Donald J. Stedman, James L. Paul, *Editors*

NEW DIRECTIONS FOR EXCEPTIONAL CHILDREN
JAMES J. GALLAGHER, *Editor-in-Chief*
Number 8, December 1981

Paperback sourcebooks in
The Jossey-Bass Social and Behavioral Sciences Series

54832

Jossey-Bass Inc., Publishers
San Francisco • Washington • London

Library
St. Joseph's College
Patchogue, N.Y. 11772

Professional Preparation for Teachers of Exceptional Children
Number 8, December 1981
 Donald J. Stedman, James L. Paul, *Editors*

New Directions for Exceptional Children Series
James J. Gallagher, *Editor-in-Chief*

Copyright © 1981 by Jossey-Bass Inc., Publishers
 and
 Jossey-Bass Limited

Copyright under International, Pan American, and Universal Copyright Conventions. All rights reserved. No part of this issue may be reproduced in any form — except for brief quotation (not to exceed 500 words) in a review or professional work — without permission in writing from the publishers.

New Directions for Exceptional Children is published quarterly by Jossey-Bass Inc., Publishers. Subscriptions, single-issue orders, change of address notices, undelivered copies, and other correspondence should be sent to *New Directions* Subscriptions, Jossey-Bass Inc., Publishers, 433 California Street, San Francisco, California 94104.

Editorial correspondence should be sent to the Editor-in-Chief, James J. Gallagher, Frank Porter Graham Child Development Center, The University of North Carolina at Chapel Hill, Chapel Hill, North Carolina 27514.

Library of Congress Catalogue Card Number LC 80-84272
International Standard Serial Number ISSN 0271-0625
International Standard Book Number ISBN 87589-824-6

Cover art by Willi Baum
Manufactured in the United States of America

Ordering Information

The paperback sourcebooks listed below are published quarterly and can be ordered either by subscription or as single copies.

Subscriptions cost $30.00 per year for institutions, agencies, and libraries. Individuals can subscribe at the special rate of $18.00 per year *if payment is by personal check.* (Note that the full rate of $30.00 applies if payment is by institutional check, even if the subscription is designated for an individual.) Standing orders are accepted.

Single copies are available at $6.95 when payment accompanies order, and *all single-copy orders under $25.00 must include payment.* (California, Washington, D.C., New Jersey, and New York residents please include appropriate sales tax.) For billed orders, cost per copy is $6.95 plus postage and handling. (Prices subject to change without notice.)

To ensure correct and prompt delivery, all orders must give either the *name of an individual* or an *official purchase order number.* Please submit your order as follows:

Subscriptions: specify series and subscription year.
Single Copies: specify sourcebook code and issue number (such as, EC8).

Mail orders for United States and Possessions, Latin America, Canada, Japan, Australia, and New Zealand to:
Jossey-Bass Inc., Publishers
433 California Street
San Francisco, California 94104

Mail orders for all other parts of the world to:
Jossey-Bass Limited
28 Banner Street
London EC1Y 8QE

New Directions for Exceptional Children Series
James J. Gallagher, *Editor-in-Chief*

EC1 *Ecology of Exceptional Children,* James J. Gallagher
EC2 *Language Intervention with Children,* Diane Bricker
EC3 *Young Exceptional Children,* James J. Gallagher
EC4 *Parents and Families of Handicapped Children,* James J. Gallagher
EC5 *Socioemotional Development,* Nicholas J. Anastasiow
EC6 *Curriculum Development for Exceptional Children,* Herbert Goldstein
EC7 *Genetics and Exceptional Children,* Kippy I. Abroms, J. W. Bennett

Contents

Foreword   1
Maynard C. Reynolds

Chapter 1. Toward Quality in Special Education   3
Training Programs
Donald J. Stedman, Roxie R. Smith, Linda D. Baucom
Strategies are presented for evaluating special education training programs and their graduates.

Chapter 2. A Process for Curricular Change in Teacher Education   19
William I. Burke, Bonnie Strickland
A review of various curriculum models and the conditions facing teacher educators are presented. The issues of governance, content, and evaluation are addressed.

Chapter 3. The North Carolina Cooperative Planning   39
Consortium: Planning for Special Education Manpower
Requirements
Cathy L. Crossland, Linda P. Blanton
An approach for cooperative planning in special education among institutions of higher education is described.

Chapter 4. Field-Based Degree Training in Special Education   51
Donald P. Bailey, Jr., David L. Lillie, James L. Paul
One university's approach to developing a field-based training is described. Discussions of collaborative planning, faculty support, program evaluation, and practica are included.

Chapter 5. Attitudes and Teacher Mainstreamed Classrooms: 73
A Review of Research
Barbara H. Wasik, Rune J. Simeonsson
The current state of knowledge regarding the preparation of teachers for mainstreamed classrooms is reviewed. Suggestions are made for future efforts.

Chapter 6. Educating Special Teachers: Inventing the Future   87
Paul F. Fendt, Marvin D. Wyne
A philosophy and strategy are presented for finding new tools to improve current approaches to the education of special teachers and plan special teacher education in the years ahead.

Index   107

Foreword

Public education in the United States has never been static. Change has always been in process because of social changes, advancements in technology, or revisions in public policy. Currently, we are in a period in which legislation and judicial reinterpretations concerning the educational rights of handicapped and other learning-disadvantaged children have placed heavy demands on public school personnel. The new policies, incorporated in the provisions of P.L. 94-142, the Education for All Handicapped Children Act of 1975, are predicated on roles and performances that classroom teachers and related personnel are ill-prepared to carry out. Thus, we are experiencing the great need to redesign teacher preparation programs to develop the capacity of public school educators to deliver on the intent and expectations of the new policies. Adequate solutions depend upon a thorough organization of the philosophy and content of teacher preparation. Much more is involved than simply adding a course or a few easy lessons on the characteristics and needs of the handicapped.

It has become clear that teacher preparation rarely has been attended to seriously in our society. This is one reason for the doubling and redoubling in recent decades of the numbers of students who are classified as requiring special education services. The burgeoning of special classes and centers resulted in the fragmentation of the schools into separate enclaves for children classified as successes or misfits. Now the press is on to reverse such negative placement policies and to increase the power of the regular school system to serve students who may not be so easy to teach.

Perhaps we should have expected educators' early responses to the new policies to be mostly expediential, such as a quick and easy set of after-school training sessions for teachers on the new policies and procedures. In some states there has been little progress beyond meeting the legal requirements of the law in order to "stay out of jail"; in other states, however, progress has been more substantial and it is these states that deserve the attention of all educators.

In this volume the authors recount the story of serious efforts—mainly in North Carolina—to meet the new challenges to teacher education. The necessary unity of "special" and "regular" teacher preparation to carry out the new policies has been recognized there, and one can read here how teacher education was expanded in range and intent. The University of North Carolina system has instituted strong programs for the planning and evaluation of teacher education on its sixteen campuses. No broader or more effective evaluation effort has ever been undertaken in higher education than by the University of North Carolina system. The story of that achievement, particularly as it relates to special education, is included here. Furthermore, North Carolina appears to be one of the states in which institutions of higher education have been able to come together for the broad and coordinated planning of special education teacher preparation in the public interest without a kind of "sovietization" in the process. Several North Carolina institutions have given strong leadership to the Dean's Grant projects, a program initiated and supported by the U.S. Department of Education to upgrade the preparation of regular classroom teachers. That leadership is also reflected in this volume.

Slowly, teacher education is emerging from the doldrums of the 1970s and from the narrow, uncoordinated specializations that characterized it in the past. In a few institutions strong movements toward quality are in process; we must hope that they will be honored and supported, and that they will eventually become the standards for the rest of us. This sourcebook provides a glimpse of some efforts that deserve such honor and emulation.

Maynard C. Reynolds
University of Minnesota

*Current economic constraints make it more important than ever
to conduct rigorous evaluations of special education training programs.
This chapter presents strategies that can be used to evaluate
baccalaureate, master's, and doctoral training programs
in special education and a strategy for assessing and
strengthening the competencies of new special education teachers.*

Toward Quality in Special Education Training Programs

Donald J. Stedman
Roxie R. Smith
Linda D. Baucom

Throughout the first half of the twentieth century the numbers of college and university training programs preparing personnel to work with children with special needs remained relatively small. However, there were increases during the 1960s and 1970s as a result of the availability of federal funds for teacher education programs. Large numbers of new undergraduate- and graduate-level programs were initiated and many existing programs were expanded significantly. This sudden growth was fueled by state legislation that expanded the range and depth of educational services for exceptional children and a corresponding increase in the demand for trained professional personnel to provide the services. A demand for doctoral-level training programs also occurred as the need intensified for researchers, leadership personnel, and faculty for training programs.

During this period of rapid growth, emphasis was placed on instructional organization, budgeting and resource development, curriculum formulation, recruiting and retraining faculty, and establishing student services—areas critical to the initiation of programs to meet the demand for trained personnel. During this unprecedented growth cycle, time and resources for a systematic process of program evaluation were lacking. As programming stabilized and a state of equilibrium was achieved, energies were channeled toward ensuring that the desired quality was present. Impetus for increased attention to evaluation came from a public demand for accountability in the expenditure of public monies, a reduced need for additional personnel in some areas, a shift in federal support from preservice to inservice programming, and the desire on the part of faculty to test whether the desired outcomes were in fact being achieved.

Prior to 1975, special education training programs relied primarily on two strategies for reviewing program quality: accreditation (as part of a total school of education review) by the National Council for Accreditation of Teacher Education and/or program approval by state departments of public education (as a component of the certification process). Some programs retained special consultants for external review; others instituted internal curriculum review committees, often a useful process but subject to the distortions associated with self-evaluation. Accreditation and program approval reviews have many similarities, both in the process and in the potential problems. Both require a period of self-study and introspection prior to the campus visit by an external review team. These reviews seek to ensure that the minimum necessary resources are present to conduct an adequate program but speak neither to the degree of quality that may be present above some minimum level of acceptability nor to the extent to which desired outcomes have been achieved. Although minimum standards may be stated, a basic set of agreed-upon dimensions and the best ways to measure them are often lacking. These processes are further weakened by an absence of specific recommendations for change that are designed to effect the desired improvement.

The assessment of special education doctoral programs has been undertaken only to obtain reputational rankings for schools of education, a process itself plagued with methodological difficulties, or as part of a cursory agency review for external funding.

This chapter describes strategies for the assessment of special education programs at the baccalaureate, master's, and doctoral levels. The methods discussed are multidimensional in scope and address shortcomings identified in generally used procedures. A strategy for assessing and strengthening the competencies of new special education teachers is also presented. Results of these evaluations provide university administrators with information to make program-improvement decisions, based on areas of strength and weakness identified by the evaluations.

Evaluating Undergraduate and Master's Degree Programs

Evaluations of existing baccalaureate and master's degree programs in special education should be statewide in scope and should focus not only upon the *quality* and *strength* of the teacher education programs but also on their *productivity* and the current *demand* for their graduates. An example of the process required to accomplish a statewide teacher education program evaluation, designed to strengthen needed programs and to discontinue weak and unneccesary programs, can be found in the strategy used by the University of North Carolina (UNC) in 1976-1978. (Detailed reports on procedures and results of the Teacher Education Review Program (Stedman, 1980; UNC General Administration, 1977, 1979, and 1981) are available by writing the authors at P.O. Box 2688, UNC General Administration, Chapel Hill, NC 27514-1509.)

The University of North Carolina Review. In 1976 there were 500 teacher education programs at undergraduate and graduate levels, including 26 teacher education specialties at fifteen of the sixteen constituent institutions of the UNC system. At the beginning of the Teacher Education Review Program (TERP), there were six undergraduate and five graduate programs in special education, including one doctoral program at the Chapel Hill campus.

Program Review. Working with a campus coordinating committee at each of the constituent institutions, TERP staff developed and disseminated questionnaire materials. The materials were designed to obtain information about the quality, productivity, and need characteristics of each of the education programs identified in the education program inventory. TERP staff then visited campuses to assist programs in understanding and completing the questionnaires.

Information returned by the institutions was reviewed by TERP staff, six major advisors, and twenty-eight special consultants to the project who reviewed the information by means of a special field-reader system. Information gathered from the institutions for each of the education programs included data on faculty, students, program, and graduates. In addition, each institution prepared a special presentation on its teacher education programs to clarify current and projected operations and priorities.

Using this method, each of the 500 programs received a strength rating of either *strong, satisfactory, marginal — needs further review,* or *weak — needs further review,* based on criteria specified and applied by each consultant in arriving at the ratings.

Productivity information provided by the institutions for each of their education programs was analyzed by TERP staff to identify the low productivity programs (an average of five or fewer graduates per year for the three-year period prior to the evaluation). The low productivity programs identified by TERP staff that were also identified by the special consultant reviewers as in need of further review were then identified as low strength/low productivity programs or tracks.

Those programs and tracks identified as having low strength and low productivity were then reviewed in relation to the demand for graduates of teacher education programs as revealed by a special study of the needs for educational personnel in North Carolina.

Each program was classified into one of several groups in accordance with their *strength, productivity,* and *need* characteristics. Initial recommendations were developed for each program based on this assessment. Information and data gathered to reach these initial recommendations were then verified with institutions before final recommendations were made.

Figure 1 shows the matrix used to classify each program and to generate specific recommendations for them.

Group A included those programs that fell into the *low strength* (weak or marginal), *low productivity, low need* cell. They were recommended for discontinuation.

Group B included those programs judged to be *low strength* and *low productivity* but for which there was an apparent need. It was recommended that a reasonable period of time be given to institutions to develop plans for their improvement. If such plans were not submitted, or if they were submitted and were judged inadequate, then the programs were recommended for discontinuation.

Group C included those programs judged to be *low strength* and *high productivity* from areas in which there was an apparent need for graduates or a demand from students for the programs. It was recommended that a reason-

Figure 1. Program Evaluation Decision Matrix

PROGRAM PRODUCTIVITY

PROGRAM STRENGTH		LOW		HIGH
		Low Need	High Need	
Needs Further Review: Weak or Marginal		A	B	C
Acceptable: Satisfactory or Strong		D		E

able period of time be given to develop plans for their improvement. Such plans often included a reduction in productivity when a high need for graduates could not be demonstrated. If such plans were not submitted, or if they were submitted and found to be inadequate, then those programs were recommended for discontinuation.

Group D included those programs judged to be *satisfactory* or *strong* and *low in productivity.* It was recommended that productivity be increased in the areas of need and that low-productivity programs in areas of low need be reviewed for possible discontinuation or cutback on the initiative of the institution.

Group E included those programs judged to be *satisfactory* or *strong* and *high productivity.* For those programs in which there was a decreasing need for graduates, it was recommended that productivity be reduced by using appropriate measures that would ensure continuation of an adequate level of quality. Programs found to be inactive were recommended for discontinuation.

Several features of the evaluation approach are worth noting:

1. The strategy selected for the implementation of TERP emphasized both process and quantitative measures in the approach to evaluating the teacher education programs. Neither process nor strictly quantitative measures alone will suffice. Both need to be gathered in an appropriate mixture in order to provide the descriptive and data-based recommendations necessary for this type of study.

2. TERP activity established a comprehensive approach to evaluating the fifteen education programs in a multicampus university system. This broad-survey approach provides for improved opportunities for comparisons between and among programs as well as the provision of a timely set of fresh data for evaluation and administrative decisions.

3. The cooperation of personnel at all levels of the teacher education programs was a positive feature from the outset. It enabled the project to move along smoothly and to remain on schedule.

4. The use of a wide variety of measures and techniques rather than dependence on one or a few meaures provided an opportunity for fairness and completeness not present in many other program evaluation approaches.

5. The development and utilization of a major-advisor's steering group and a field-reader system made available a wide variety of experienced specialists to assist in the gathering, evaluation, and interpretation of information. The use of a large group of special content consultants provided an external review feature not usually present in a review of existing programs by the central staff of a multicampus system engaged in program evaluation.

6. TERP activity was accomplished within a twelve-month period, which helped avoid the problem of too much elapsed time between information gathering and information analyses and recommendations.

7. The program presentations by each institution's teacher education program staff included a wealth of information of deep concern to the leadership of the teacher education programs in the fifteen constituent institutions of the university.

The most frequently cited barriers to improved program operations were:

1. A need for a forum within which improved communications and joint program planning and development might take place among the teacher education programs in the university.
2. A need for a more orderly and effective method for programs to be responsive to the planning and training needs of the schools and other organizations in their regions and around the state.
3. A need for opportunities for faculty development and professional renewal.
4. A need for more systematic and comprehensive information on manpower needs in the state.
5. A need to explore more aggressively the needs and opportunities for interinstitutional program development.
6. A need for clarity in certification procedures, standards, and sources of authority for the licensing of teachers.
7. A need to explore and more fully capitalize on nontraditional markets for teachers.
8. A need for authorization of more master's programs to meet mounting pressures for inservice educational services in certain regions of the state, especially special education.

Results. Sixty-three of the 500 teacher education programs included in the review were discontinued because of inadequate strength, productivity, and need. An additional 34 programs were combined with similar programs on the same campus to improve their effectiveness. Eighty-seven underwent significant improvement and programs with high need for graduates were strengthened and assigned high priority on their own campus for new or reallocated resources. Twenty-six new teacher education programs in high-need areas have been authorized by the university since completion of the review.

Implications for Special Education. One of the important results of the North Carolina review was to underscore the needs of special education programs, especially at the master's degree level. The review activity was a major determinant in the strengthening and expansion of special education teacher training programs in North Carolina between 1976 and 1981. The productivity of special education programs increased by 35 percent; the number of programs increased from six to fourteen at the baccalaureate level and from five to ten at the master's level. The priority assigned to special education programs on all campuses increased significantly as administrators became aware of the need for special educators and the corresponding need to strengthen special education programs. Even more importantly, the review pinpointed weak and unnecessary programs from which resources could be moved to strengthen special education.

If quality is to be improved, both in special education programs and in their graduates, then a comprehensive review of all teacher education programs must be undertaken. If reviews focus only on special education programs, program weaknesses may be identified but few remedies are possible if new resources are not available. Comprehensive evaluation ensures a fair review with an equitable redistribution of resources based on program effectiveness, student demand, and a need for the graduates of certain programs.

Evaluating Doctoral Programs

Evaluating the quality of doctoral programs in special education requires a strategy that can be employed at the national level. Most states have a need for only one or two doctoral programs, making intrastate review and comparisons impractical. The existing strategies of accreditation and reputational ranking are inadequate for the reasons noted earlier. What is needed is a multidimensional approach to evaluation that (1) has an agreed-upon set of standards for judging quality, (2) has carefully specified means for measuring standards, (3) includes involvement of program faculties and students in data collection, and (4) provides a method of gathering information that can be translated into doctoral program activities.

Review Process. In 1976, Clark and others developed a strategy for assessing program quality and applied it to several arts and sciences programs. Although this approach proved to be valid and reliable for programs preparing researchers, certain adaptations were necessary to accommodate the unique characteristics of professional education programs. Professional training programs prepare individuals to deliver specific services to benefit mankind through the solution of real-life situations and the curriculum must reflect this. A substantial body of knowledge, identifiable skills and techniques, and the norms of the profession must be learned by students through a mixture of didactic instruction, carefully supervised practicum experiences, and appropriate behavioral modeling by extensive interaction between the students and the faculty. Special education doctoral programs prepare teachers, researchers, and other leadership personnel by utilizing this professional instructional model.

A special study (Smith, 1979) was conducted to adapt the multidimensional approach used by Clark and others for use with special education doctoral programs. The study was conducted in two phases. In the first phase the characteristics considered important for judging program strength were identified and the most appropriate ways to measure them were specified. The results of this activity permitted formulation of evaluation instrumentation that was then field tested with twenty-five special education doctoral programs as part of the second phase of the study. Through this process, satisfactory levels of validity and reliability for applying the multidimensional approach to professional training programs were established.

Phase I: Formulation of the Evaluation Instrument. Two groups were utilized in the instrumentation development process—doctoral program chairpersons and an expert panel comprised of individuals who were nationally prominent persons in the field of special education. Chairpersons were selected for their current experience and knowledge related to special educational doctoral program operations. The comparison group was constituted to ensure that an adequate historical perspective was maintained and parochialism avoided, thereby reducing the potential for sample bias and further ensuring the validity of the results.

The two groups were first asked to identify the information they believed was necessary to make a judgment about the strength of a special education doctoral program. A range of possibilities was provided, utilizing a format adapted from materials developed by the Educational Testing Service. Categories included characteristics of faculty, students, resources, and program operations. Significant differences in the ratings of the two groups were noted and only those dimensions rated important or essential by both groups were used. An analysis of the characteristics identified by each group as essential revealed few significant differences. Although the panel of experts believed that fewer items were needed to make decisions, a high level of concurrence was found. When those items that both groups rated as important or essential were ranked and correlated, a moderate to strong relationship between the order of the responses of the two groups was also found, further indicating that the relevant characteristics had been identified.

Faculty characteristics that were identified included three background dimensions (academic training, variety of specialties, and teaching experience), four process dimensions (research activity, concern for students, teaching effectiveness, and program involvement), and three output dimensions (research productivity, teaching honors, and morale). Student characteristics that were identified included two background dimensions (ability and career interests), one process dimension (involvement), and seven output dimensions (knowledge, skills, professional accomplishments, placement, perceptions of quality, satisfaction, and morale). Resource characteristics that were identified included financial support, library holdings, equipment and facilities, off-campus resources, institutional mission, and institutional strengths. Characteristics of program operations included administrative activities as well as those related to the teaching–learning process.

Although most of the characteristics identified by the special education program chairpersons and expert panel members were the same as those identified by the arts and sciences deans in Clark's (1974) study, there were some differences. In arts and sciences, the deans identified a "concern for undergraduate education" as a characteristic of faculty quality, while only the special education persons identified a "variety of specialties among the faculty" as essential for judging faculty strength. Only special educators identified student involvement in professional affairs and job placement of graduates as indicators of student quality and the availability and utilization of off-campus resources (internship sites and adjunct faculty) as indicators of the strength of the resources. Only arts and sciences people saw the availability of classroom and office space as an important characteristic.

Arts and sciences people identifed five characteristics as essential for making judgments about the quality of program operations. These were provision for the welfare of the faculty, provision for assistance for new and young faculty, job placement of graduates, efficiency of degree production, and size of the program. Only special educators identified support staff for the academic program, provision for meeting individual needs of students, personal and academic freedom, recent innovations, and the program decision-making structure as essential characteristics. Many of the differences that were found reflect the unique aspects of a professional training program that distinguish them from academic programs in the arts and sciences.

Having identified forty-five characteristics important for judging the strength of special education doctoral programs, the two groups were then asked to indicate the best means for measuring these characteristics. Significant differences in the ratings of the two groups were noted and only those measures rated *good* or *very good* were used. An analysis of the differences in the measures selected by each group revealed few significant differences. Although the panel of experts believed fewer measures were critical to the assessment process, a high level of concurrence was again found, indicating that the best means of measuring the essential characteristics had been identified.

Measures of faculty characteristics that were selected included number of publications, teacher-effectiveness ratings, ratings of faculty concern for students, faculty satisfaction, and evidence of other professional productivity. Measures of student characteristics included number of publications, employment records, student satisfaction, knowledge and skill gains, and evidence of other professional productivity. Measures of resource characteristics included appropriateness of courses, internships, and the advisement process; clarity of purposes and plans; student, faculty, and alumni satisfaction; degree of flexibility; and degree of input by the community of interests into program operations.

Phase II: Field Test. In the second phase of the study, a survey using sixty-one of the seventy-nine preferred measures was developed. The items that were deleted required ratings by a visiting team of experts and did not meet the implementation criteria. Following development of the protocols, an additional analysis was undertaken. Items to be included were reviewed with respect to the summary of doctoral-level special education degree program requirements described by Kirk (1957). The questionnaires were also reviewed to ensure that the minimum necessary components would be assessed for a special education doctoral program that trained administrators, college and university teachers, and researchers. Such a program has been described by Gallagher (1959). It was concluded that all aspects except admissions criteria would be included.

A field test of the evaluation strategy was then conducted with twenty-five special education doctoral programs to ensure the feasibility of the process and establish a satisfactory level of reliability. The twenty-five programs were located in all regions of the nation, including public and private institutions and small, medium, and large programs. All doctoral faculty members, current students, and graduates from the previous five years were analyzed and a format for presenting results was developed, utilizing a design similar to that reported by Clark and others (1976). The format permitted a comparison of a program's mean response on any given item with those of other participating programs. By plotting all of the items on the grid, a profile of a program's strengths and weaknesses was created. A sample profile is shown in Table 1. Separate profiles were generated for faculty, students, and graduates.

Each program participating in the evaluation was provided with profiles in the following seven areas:
- Faculty perceptions of program strength
- Student perceptions of program strength
- Graduate perceptions of program strength
- Faculty, student, and graduate perceptions of program strength
- Student perceptions of faculty characteristics
- Graduate perceptions of faculty characteristics
- Student and graduate perceptions of faculty characteristics.

Results. An analysis of trends across all the participating programs revealed that graduates perceive their programs to be stronger than faculty or students do, probably due in part to having successfully negotiated the program. Faculty can see both strengths and weaknesses in their programs, whereas students and graduates appear to have an overall perception of a program's

Table 1. Faculty, Student, and Graduate Perceptions of Special Education Doctoral Program Strength

Institution: Sample

	LOWEST	25th %ILE	MEDIAN	75th %ILE	HIGHEST
Objectives clearly stated	2.92	2.36	2.09	1.75	1.11
Degree requirements clearly stated	2.35	1.84	1.64	1.43	1.00
Requirements reflect objectives	2.89	2.22	2.00	1.77	1.30
Many points of view tolerated	2.47	2.11	1.75	1.49	1.36
Student advisement adequate	3.22	2.14	1.86	1.71	1.26
Common core of courses and experiences	2.70	2.11	1.63	1.43	1.16
Training matched to individual needs	2.42	1.92	1.67	1.52	1.19
Variety of relevant courses available	2.40	1.98	1.74	1.55	1.45
Coursework in related fields encouraged	2.52	1.88	1.82	1.60	1.22
Practicum experiences selected for individual	2.45	1.93	1.61	1.41	1.26
Library and media resources adequate	2.61	1.88	1.70	1.36	1.12
Practicum sites plentiful and varied	2.92	2.10	1.93	1.71	1.43
Student input in administration welcomed	3.03	2.36	2.14	1.78	1.00
Opportunities to work with faculty	1.98	1.70	1.44	1.30	1.00
Research activities emphasized in latter part	2.41	2.04	1.80	1.60	1.22
Freedom to select dissertation topic	2.09	1.54	1.35	1.24	1.00
Dissertation committees helpful	2.76	1.98	1.82	1.68	1.51
Coursework provides useful knowledge	2.07	1.95	1.68	1.52	1.17
Practicum experiences provide needed skills	2.07	1.85	1.56	1.40	1.18
Assistantship experiences useful	1.81	1.68	1.52	1.46	1.00
Adequate enrichment activities scheduled	3.08	2.60	2.25	1.89	1.58
Program prepares researchers/scholars	3.00	2.49	2.20	1.82	1.20
Program prepares college/university teachers	2.08	1.86	1.68	1.46	1.24
Program prepares other practitioners	3.20	2.38	2.12	1.76	1.37

strength as either satisfactory or unsatisfactory. Graduates and students were found to have a high degree of concurrence regarding the quality of program faculty as either strong or weak.

Analyses of demographic and professional characteristics of the responding faculty, students, and graduates of the twenty-five participating programs revealed a fairly positive profile of special education doctoral training programs across the nation. The faculty as a whole are quite productive in the following areas: publishing; competing successfully for external funds; holding office in state, regional, and national professional organizations; and making presentations and providing consultation. Most, however, are white males. Programs, therefore, should direct attention to their recruitment efforts in order to attract more women and minorities to their faculties. Overall, the students have favorable perceptions of their training programs and most would recommend their program to others. While over half of the students are women, few minorities were represented among this group and recruitment efforts should be intensified in this area. Graduates of the programs present a favorable employment picture. Many are professionally productive and already contributing to this field.

Implications. The multidimensional strategy described here for assessing the strengths of special education doctoral programs has been demonstrated to be both valid and reliable. More importantly, it is useful for both administrative and program planning. Designed to address difficulties present in other methods, it provides programs with specific information regarding strengths and weaknesses. Its information is timely and relevant in that results reflect the current status of a program and can be regularly updated. Further, since those within the program's community of interests have been actively involved in the data-gathering process, improvements that have been pinpointed may as a result be easier to implement.

Strengthening the Competencies of Special Education Teachers

In addition to evaluating special education programs at all degree levels, it is also important to regularly assess the professional performance of graduates and to provide ongoing educational support to help ensure their effectiveness. The most critical period of professional development is the initial period of work when a new teacher begins his or her profession while continuing to build skills on the job through inservice and continuing education activities. An effective method of accomplishing this is through technical-assistance programs.

Technical Assistance. Technical assistance (TA) is a process by which information is transferred from one organization or individual (the TA agent) to another (the client). TA agents and services have existed in some fields for decades, such as county agents and extension services in agriculture (Rogers, 1962). More recently, TA systems have begun to appear in educational settings as a way of meeting legislative requirements, responding to the increased emphasis on the quality of services and accountability, and moving toward creative and nontraditional strategies for delivering educational services.

TA is recommended as a framework for assessing and strengthening the competencies of beginning teachers, including special education teachers. In North Carolina this process is being considered for use during the three-year period of initial certification of teachers (Quality Assurance Program, 1981). Its goal is to assist new teachers in identifying their competencies and needs and to provide resources so that teachers can address their identified needs. Its intent is to be constructive, not punitive; needs are identified so that they can be remedied and the TA system provides the resources for remedial activities.

TA Agent. The process begins with the identification of a TA agent in each of the educational programs of the state. In one region, the agent might be affiliated with a college or a university; in another, the TA agent might be a public or private agency separate from the educational system. There are at least three common characteristics that all TA agents must demonstrate in order to serve teachers effectively. First, the TA agent must be independent of the clients' organization, the public schools. The TA staff must be free to deliver services without having to seek approval from the public schools or be limited by the school's budgetary constraints. Second, the TA agent must be competent to either address the teachers' needs directly or to identify and "broker" other resources to meet the needs. Third, the TA agent must be able to establish and maintain a relationship of trust with teachers who are being served. The teachers must understand that the TA agent's goal is to help them strengthen their capabilities. They must recognize that the TA agent will not participate in any way in future decisions regarding the teacher, such as matters related to employment or certification. Only when such an atmosphere of trust is established will teachers feel free to be candid in helping to identify their own needs as well as their competencies.

TA Process. Technical assistance can be conceptualized as a five-step process (compare Lillie and Black, 1976; Stedman, 1975; Trohanis, 1980). First, the TA agent must become thoroughly knowledgeable about the local school systems whose teachers are served. The agent must understand the schools' overall mission, long-term goals, work load and patterns, and time frames. Only then will the agent be able to properly understand and assess the teachers' individual concerns and needs. In addition to becoming thoroughly familiar with the school system, the TA agent must also orient all beginning teachers to the process of TA, explaining that assistance is available and clarifying how it can help them.

Second, the TA agent and the beginning teacher together assess the teacher's strengths and needs. The TA agent conducts a structured interview with the teacher to help pinpoint discrepancies between the teacher's current competencies and the teacher's desired competencies. In order to validate the information obtained through the interview, the TA agent may seek data from other sources, such as observations of the teacher in the classroom, reports from students or parents, pupil-outcome measures, or self-evaluation reports by the teacher.

Third, once the teacher's needs are identified, the TA agent and the teacher must decide together which needs to address first, how they will be addressed, and within what time frame. An agreement is prepared and signed, stating in clear and unambiguous language exactly what will be done for the teacher. It is desirable for an administrator in the school system, such as the principal, to sign the agreement as well, indicating the school's endorsement and support.

Fourth, the TA agent systematically delivers resources to the teacher or arranges for the services to be provided by some other person or organization. The resources can come from the agency and its own staff or from other sources. The TA agent often provides services directly through a personal, on-site consultation with the teacher. Alternately, the TA agent may use other strategies, such as reviewing and critiquing written materials and products, arranging for peer consultation, conducting a workshop, arranging for the teacher to visit some other teacher or school, or searching for needed information. It is crucial that the TA system mold its services according to the teacher's identified needs, not vice versa. That is, the TA system responds to a teacher's needs rather than offering a predetermined selection of services.

The fifth step, evaluation of the TA, occurs both during and after service delivery. A written questionnaire can be used to determine the answers to several questions. Were the services delivered as the agreement specified? Did the services help the teacher? Was the teacher satisfied? After the evaluation is completed, the teacher may request another needs assessment and the TA process can be recycled.

TA Features and Benefits. Two features of the TA process make it appear promising. First, a relationship of trust must undergird the assessment of the teacher's needs; the trust is bolstered by the fact that the TA agent is independent of the school system and clearly separate from future decision making regarding the teacher's employment or certification status. Second, the same agent both identifies the teacher's needs and delivers or coordinates the delivery of resources to meet the needs. Thus, the risk of slippage is minimized; such risk would be greater if one agency identified the needs and a separate agency addressed them.

The TA system design permits effective budgetary management and economic controls, since the technical assistance is developed, delivered, and coordinated by the agency's own staff members. Essentially containing the activity within the TA system itself, rather than deploying a complex network of outside consultants, presents a manageable and efficient system for delivery of services to new teachers.

Besides benefitting the teachers directly, the technical assistance activity also benefits teacher education programs by generating information on the strengths and needs of their graduates. The information can be shared with the colleges and universities, and if it is provided in sufficient detail, it can be used by colleges and universities in program planning and development activities as a guide toward needed revisions and tailoring curricula to provide a balanced program of quality preservice training.

Conclusions

Given the current economic constraints being placed on teacher education programs by enrollment declines and eroding federal funds, it is more important than ever to undertake a rigorous and comprehensive evaluation of all existing programs in teacher education and of graduates of these programs. The processes described herein can be adapted anywhere and applied at various program levels to evaluate both preservice and inservice teacher education activities. This will not only serve to review and strengthen current special education training programs but will also provide higher education administrators with sources of funds for reallocation of existing resources from unproductive or unnecessary programs to needy special education teacher training programs.

References

Clark, M. J. *The Assessment of Quality in Ph.D. Programs*. Princeton, N.J.: Educational Testing Service, 1974.

Clark, M. J., Hartnett, R., and Baird, L. *Assessing Dimensions of Quality in Doctoral Education*. Princeton, N.J.: Educational Testing Service, 1976.

Gallagher, J. J. "Advanced Graduate Training in Special Education." *Exceptional Children,* 1959, *26* (1), 104-109.

Kirk, S. "A Doctor's Degree Program in Special Education." *Exceptional Children,* 1957, *24* (2), 50-55.

Lillie, D. L., and Black, T. "Principles and Procedures in Technical Assistance: An Approach to Educational Change." *Educational Technology,* 1976, *16,* 33-36.

Quality Assurance Program. *Liaison Committee Report*. Raleigh, N.C.: Quality Assurance Program, 1981.

Rogers, E. *Diffusions of Innovations.* New York: Free Press, 1962.

Smith, R. R. "Adapting a Multidimensional Approach to the Assessment of Program Quality in Special Education Doctoral Programs." Unpublished doctoral dissertation, University of North Carolina at Chapel Hill, 1979.

Stedman, D. J. "The Technical Assistance System: A New Organizational Form for Improving Education." In M. C. Reynolds (Ed.), *National Technical Assistance Systems in Special Education.* Minneapolis, Minn.: Leadership Training Institute/Special Education, 1975.

Stedman, D. J. *Improving Teacher Education: Academic Program Review.* Atlanta, Ga.: Southern Regional Education Board, 1980.

Trohanis, P. O. "Technical Assistance: An Innovative Approach to Building New Partnerships in Continuing and Inservice Education." *Educational Technology,* 1980, *20,* 30-36.

University of North Carolina, General Administration. *The Education and Training of Teachers and Other Educational Personnel in the University of North Carolina: A Review and Evaluation of Teacher Education in the University of North Carolina* (Report 2). Chapel Hill, N.C.: Teacher Education Review Program, 1977.

University of North Carolina, General Administration. *The Education and Training of Teachers and Other Educational Personnel in the University of North Carolina: Report on the Status of the Implementation of the TERP Recommendations* (Report 4). Chapel Hill, N.C.: Teacher Education Review Program, 1979.

University of North Carolina, General Administration. *The Education and Training of Teachers and Other Educational Personnel in the University of North Carolina: Final Report on the Review of Teacher Education Programs in the University of North Carolina, 1976-1981* (Report 5). Chapel Hill, N.C.: Teacher Education Review Program, 1981.

Donald J. Stedman is associate vice-president for academic affairs of the University of North Carolina, and a professor of education at the University of North Carolina at Chapel Hill.

Roxie R. Smith is assistant dean of the School of Education at Northwestern University.

Linda D. Baucom is research assistant in the office of the president of the University of North Carolina.

The needs of exceptional children have created implications for the future directions of teacher education curricula.

A Process for Curricular Change in Teacher Education

William I. Burke
Bonnie Strickland

"If teachers are the keystone of the school system, their adequacy must be judged in quality as well as in numbers. This immediately leads to questions about their preparation" (Eurich, 1960, p. 154). It is these questions that we will examine in the course of this chapter. Specifically, our focus is the curriculum and the planning of the curriculum for preservice teachers who will teach exceptional children in regular classrooms. The chapter is divided into three sections: concepts, assumptions, and questions; the conditions facing teacher education; and a proposed curriculum.

Concepts, Assumptions, and Questions

The curriculum we refer to is that for teacher education. While we acknowledge that there are various definitions of curriculum, we choose to use the definition of Saylor and others (1981, p. 78), since we assume that it is more comprehensive than others. "Curriculum is . . . a plan for providing sets of learning opportunities for persons to be educated. Our definition . . . dictates that the curriculum anticipates the provision of learning opportunities for a particular set of objectives and a particular population. That is, the curriculum is not just any plan; it is a total plan for the program of a particular educational setting." We agree with Hirst (1974, p. 16) that "if curriculum planning is a matter of planning means to specified ends, and an educational curriculum therefore serves educational ends, the clearer we are about those ends and their nature the more adequate the planning can be."

In planning a curriculum for teachers, educators must rely upon various sources of data. If the curriculum is to meet the needs of the learner, in this case the teacher, and thus provide opportunities for the teacher to develop the knowledge, attitudes, and skills involved in teaching, we maintain that the following sources constitute the critical data for planning. These sources include society and culture, selection and organization of knowledge, human development, learning theory, legal and extralegal factors, professional opinion, and resource acquisition and allocation. If the definition of curriculum is assumed, an educator who is planning curriculum should consider the following questions:

1. Who is the learner? Using data about the society and culture, we can gain insight about the environment from which the learner comes. Knowledge of human development allows the teacher to better understand the social, emotional, physical, and intellectual development of the learner.

2. What shall the teacher teach the learner? In part, this question requires that the teacher have an understanding of the specific discipline or subject that forms the content of the interaction between teacher and learner. A teacher should understand the structure of the particular discipline or subject so as to "gain a coherent picture of the subject, get a glimpse of the vast reaches of knowledge, feel the cutting edge of disciplined training, and discover the satisfactions of the scholarly habit of mind (so that if he becomes a teacher, he can communicate something of this spirit to others)" (Conant, 1963, p. 106).

3. How does the learner learn? In part, this question requires that the teacher have an understanding of learning theory and the related theories of cognition and motivation. We accept as axiomatic the idea that each learner is unique. If this is so, we assume that a teacher should realize that learners learn knowledge, skills, and attitudes in distinctively different ways. Consequently, a teacher should be armed with an understanding of human learning so as to guide his or her actions in developing teaching strategies designed to enhance the learning of individual learners.

Four of the above sources (society and culture, knowledge, human development, and learning theory) constitute what we consider to be the major sources of data in that they provide us with information about particular learners. However, education exists within a political and social context. Before teaching occurs, the curriculum planners should consider those factors

that shape the context in which teaching may occur. These factors (legal and extralegal, professional opinion, and resources) help to determine the following questions:
- Who shall be taught?
- Who shall teach?
- What shall be taught and to whom?
- What resources exist?

The legal factors provide planners with information about the public mandates regarding the participants, content, resources, and even the nature of instruction. In essence, they form the formal parameters of the educational setting. Extralegal factors such as public opinion or interest groups influence the climate in which education occurs. These extralegal factors often form the basis for legal mandates. A case in point is P.L. 94-142 and corresponding state legislation. These laws came about because of the growing public realization that all children did not have access to a free and appropriate education. The parents of exceptional children, professional educators involved with exceptional children, and other interest groups raised the consciousness level of the public regarding the rights of exceptional children. Curriculum planners who do not examine (or examine only lightly) these extralegal factors may find that their curricula are not responsive to the needs of the society. In such cases, education may be viewed by the clients (for example, learners and parents) as being reactionary instead of anticipatory.

Professional opinion from learned societies (for example, the National Council of Mathematics Teachers) can guide planners in determining what shall be taught and how the learner shall be taught. The learned societies provide a convenient means for planners to gain access to the various and often latest ideas about a discipline or subject. Furthermore, the recommendations of such societies usually represent the collective thinking of the group. These recommendations provide planners with the empirical support for their curriculum rationales.

Finally, how resources will be allocated and how new resources might be acquired are important questions for any curriculum planner. This source of data enables the planner to grasp the constraints as well as the potential of a curriculum. In reality, planners may wish to neglect this source of data; to do so, however, may lead the planner and others to unrealistic expectations that dampen or even nullify the critical thesis of the proposed curriculum. Perhaps of even greater importance is the need for the planner to exercise the principle of parsimony or economy. Curriculum plans that require a highly complex resource provision may impede the demonstration of the effectiveness of such curricula. Examples of such curricula in teacher education were the Elementary Education Model programs funded by the Office of Education in the

1960s (Burdin and Lanzillotti, 1969). These curricula required resources far beyond what decision makers were apparently willing to allocate. The purpose of each curriculum was the improvement of the education of elementary teachers. As a result of the complex resource requirements, these curricula were never implemented. It is true that a by-product of such endeavors did aid in the germination of ideas concerning teacher education reform; the by-product, however, was not the principal purpose.

Conditions

In this section we will outline the conditions that will necessitate change in the teacher education curriculum if regular classroom teachers are to provide for the learning needs of exceptional children (Drew and Buchanan, 1979). Historically, curriculum changes have been fostered by social and philosophical shifts in perspective as a result of demands by significant groups within the society and an increase of the public consciousness brought about by shifts in the political hegemony. A few examples of such changes may further illustrate our point. In 1893 the Committee of Ten stated that one of the basic purposes of the high school was to prepare students for the university. Thus, they implied that a high school education was only for the few people who could attend a university. Supposedly, the Committee of Ten was reflecting the mood of the public. However, twenty-five years later another National Education Association (NEA) committee, the Committee on the Reorganization of the Secondary Schools, repudiated the work of the previous NEA committee by advocating that high school prepare people for life. Thus, they proposed that all adolescents have the opportunity to acquire a high school education, since it would better equip them for life. Such a change was the result of the demands of immigrants and the working class as well as the change in the labor needs of an industrial society. Similar changes in curricula can be observed in the area of civil rights for minority groups such as blacks, women, and senior citizens. We assume that many of these changes in curricula resulted because education did not anticipate in its curriculum the needs of various segments of society. We also propose that the concern for the educational rights of exceptional children, which resulted in a public mandate, occurred because education, and in particular the curriculum, did not reflect the needs of these children.

Impetus for Change in Teacher Education. P.L. 94-142, the Education for All Handicapped Children Act of 1975, required unprecedented change in the way in which exceptional children were to be educated and thus in the responsibilities of public school personnel, primarily teachers. In extending new and specific educational rights to exceptional children and their parents, P.L. 94-142 extended new and specific responsibilities to public school personnel and subsequently to programs that prepare teachers. The need for change in the curriculum of teacher education programs increased after the enactment of P.L. 94-142 as a result of many factors, including the following: The service delivery system within many public school systems was being reorganized based on the concept of least-restrictive environment; legislative provisions that laid the groundwork for involvement of higher education in public school reorganization were included in P.L. 94-142; curricular needs, as identified by other agencies, were imposing increased pressure on the existing structure of teacher education; and provisions of federal assistance for the reorganization of teacher education programs were made available.

Federal Assistance for Higher Education. Special education constituencies at the federal level attempted to promote change in teacher education curricula that would incorporate training of regular classroom teachers to accommodate a wide range of abilities among their students in the regular classrooms. The Bureau of Education for the Handicapped, now the Office of Special Education, has provided grants to deans of schools, colleges, or departments of education for the purpose of investigating alternative solutions to the various problems emanating from the need for change in teacher preparation programs (Behrens and Grosenick, 1978). These grants, called Dean's Grants since the deans are required to serve as the project directors, are primarily designed to stimulate change in the curriculum of programs that prepare teachers to work in regular classroom situations. Although the purpose of these grants is specific to curricula that are necessary to prepare teachers working with exceptional children in regular classrooms, at the same time an opportunity has been afforded to restructure or redesign the basic training program for teachers, thus assimilating an otherwise patchwork curriculum into a clear curricular framework. Considering the increasing allegations that teacher training programs are not meeting the preparation needs of teachers (Howsam and others, 1976) and the availability of funding to explore alternative methods, many universities and colleges have viewed the Dean's Grants as a means of addressing the complex issues involved in changing generic aspects of teacher education programs.

Components of Curriculum Reform. Most change projects in teacher education, regardless of the way in which they were conceptualized, have had similar purposes. The major purpose is to develop a training program that prepares educators to offer effective instruction to students. The goals of most projects have centered on the following objectives:
- Revising curriculum content
- Legitimizing the new curriculum
- Evaluating the curriculum
- Producing new curriculum materials.

Fundamental to the attainment of these objectives has been the increased awareness of the need for change in teacher education faculties. It is our intent to review the first three objectives, since we believe they represent the major components of curriculum reform.

Revising Curriculum Content. In addressing the problem of reorganization of curricula to facilitate the preparation of teachers for mainstreaming, many models have been developed. Primarily, these models consist of three different curriculum approaches: the addition of courses, integration of new content into an existing curricular framework, and total revision of the existing curriculim content. Each of these frameworks will be discussed briefly.

Some universities have responded to the need for special education training for regular educators by adding a new course or track to the requirements of the already existing teacher education program. This approach is relatively simple to achieve but tends to perpetuate the patchwork type of curriculum. Scriven (1976) has indicated that improvement in teacher education will not be achieved by any add-on approach; rather, efforts should be toward radical rather than patchwork reform. This approach also has the effect of maintaining special education as a separate entity and a separate body of knowledge rather than relating it to other curricula within the preparation program.

A more desirable approach to curricular revision is the identification of new content that should be included in teacher education programs and the review of the basic training program to determine logically where the new material should be included. This approach has the advantage of promoting an integrated organizational approach to mainstreaming but assumes that the existing curricular framework or structure is appropriate.

The final method is by total curriculum revision. This method has been considered by many to provide the best solution to the ills that plague preparation programs (Martin, 1976; Meyer, 1979; Ryan, 1980; Scriven, 1976). Total curriculum revision has been addressed in two ways: a mandated approach and an incremental approach. Both result in a more relevant, efficient curriculum but they begin at opposite points.

The first method of total revision involves an institutional mandate for change. A decision is made that the entire training program will be reviewed and, if necessary, dismantled. The advantage of this approach is that the mandated change is accomplished instantaneously and everyone is aware that the change has occurred and what the parameters of that change entail. The disadvantage of the approach is that it cannot guarantee the effective implementation of the new curriculum by resistant faculty members.

The other approach to total curriculum revision is on an incremental basis (Turnbull and Strickland, 1978). This method utilizes a systematic approach that includes preparation of small numbers of faculty in the area of attitudes and staff development and pursues a negotiation strategy on course content with these faculty members. This method, rather than starting at the top, begins with each faculty member, builds support for the changes, and effects such changes on an incremental basis. The disadvantage of this method is that institutionalization of curricular change becomes more difficult when support for the change has been negotiated on an individual basis rather than on a mandated, all-inclusive basis.

Identification of Appropriate Curricular Content. Since P.L. 94-142 provided the mandate for change in public schools and an impetus for change in teacher education, it might be expected that proposed changes in curriculum would be reflective of the provisions therein. Thus, in all three approaches to curriculum revision there has been an attempt to identify the capabilities teachers must have if they are to perform in accordance with the policies of P.L. 94-142 (Behrens, 1980).

As might be expected, the objectives of most projects have been specific to the task of curriculum change for regular education teachers rather than to the task of a general overhaul of the teacher education program. However, many universities have found that in order to address the problem effectively, more generic problems that plague teacher education programs and curricula have had to be addressed. In regard to curricular content, the primary problem encountered is the lack of a valid knowledge base that indicates what teachers need to know (Corrigan, 1978; Lucas, 1978). According to Ryan (1980), there is no clear body of knowledge to indicate what characteristics of curricula foster the development of a good teacher. Thus, there is no existing reliable structure within which to place or by which to test the value of a new or modified curriculum. Implicit in the movement to change the curriculum of teacher education programs is the assumption that the new content is more valuable than what it will replace. With no established rules to determine what is valuable content and what is not, it is difficult to justify the preference of one body of knowledge to the exclusion of another to all factions within a teacher education faculty.

The lack of a valid knowledge base has polarized those constituencies most involved in curriculum development. At one extreme, teachers and many teacher educators have stressed performance-based instruction as if classroom success were independent of mastery of theoretical knowledge (Lucas, 1978). These constituencies prefer training programs based on practical skills. Others emphasize the need for prospective teachers to engage in the discovery and application of theoretical knowledge (Smith, 1969). Smith (1980, p. 4), in his description of the state of the teacher education curriculum, stated that "this cleavage has given rise to divisive orientations in faculties and to discontent among students with pedagogy as a professional study. This condition need not have developed, for when knowledge is properly understood it is clear that the path from knowledge to skills is continuous." Striking an equitable balance between the two extremes appears difficult, given the present structure of teacher education and the current time constraints on preparing teachers (Corrigan, 1978).

In addition, there exists a problem in the organization of curricular content of preparation programs. Smith (1980, p. 4) illustrates this problem in his review of the competency-based movement and Conant's position on professional education content. He concluded that "neither one recognized the disarray of pedagogical knowledge and the necessity of assembling and sifting the knowledge from all sources as a prior condition to formulating objectives of instruction and training." Because of the disorganization currently apparent in the structure and content of teacher education curriculum, it is difficult to discern how a valid knowledge base will emerge.

In summary, there appears to be little substantive evidence of what should be the structure and content of the curriculum and on what basis that curriculum should be determined. Also, there is little apparent organization of the existing curriculum. Even so, proposals for restructuring teacher education curriculum have spawned a proliferation of competencies needed by regular educators to accommodate exceptional children in regular classrooms.

The preference for competency-based restructuring apparently resulted from an increasing need for accountability and quality control (Denmark and others, 1980; Iriarte, 1980). There was, in addition, a recognized need to identify a valid body of knowledge in teacher education programs (Howsam and others, 1976; Iriarte, 1980; Lucas, 1978). For many, the identification of specific competencies accomplished this goal. If one considers the knowledge base to be comprised of both "ordinary" as well as "scientific" knowledge, then the expectations that society holds for teachers (namely, P.L. 94-142) may be important in developing competencies. Reynolds and others suggested an approach to competency development through role analysis (*A Common Body of Practice* . . . , 1980).

The competency-based and performance-based models of restructuring teacher education programs are not as popular with those who feel that there is inadequate research to relate certain teaching behaviors to certain teaching outcomes (Stedman, 1980). Since there is little research to guide the development of competencies, most decisions regarding the characteristics, behaviors, and standards for competency have been based on professional biases, intuitions, and experiences (Grotelueschen and Lahti, 1978; Rader, 1978; West and Bates, 1978).

Legitimizing Curricular Change. Regardless of the curriculum approach used, teacher preparation programs have been faced with the need to reorganize in a timely fashion (Reynolds, 1978a). However, in most Dean's Grant projects, the experience has been that conceptualization and planning for change have been easier to accomplish than change itself (Behrens and Grosenick, 1978). In attempting to legitimize proposed curriuclar changes, personnel of Dean's Grant projects have encountered problems regarding faculty resistance to change within the existing structure of curriculum and difficulty in achieving institutionalization of proposed curricular change.

Reynolds (1978b) has indicated that the first goal in any change program is to make faculty members aware of the need for change. He reported that some of the Dean's Grant projects have had more success in this area than others. Hall (1978) noted that faculty awareness of the need for change does not necessarily indicate that faculty are willing to change. This situation is exemplified in the description of one university at which faculty had systematically moved forward to an awareness level but, because no further action was taken by the administration, the faculty gradually lost interest in the proposed change and became highly concentrated at a level at which there was little involvement in the change effort and little effort to become involved. In many colleges and universities where a mandated change strategy has been incorporated at the beginning of the Dean's Grant project, some faculty members and administrators were still reported to be actively resistant to the concept of change two years after the change had been mandated (Hall, 1978).

Resistance to change on the part of faculty may be a result of many factors, including the potential threat to the academic freedom of the faculty when curricular change is proposed, the perceived lack of value of the new procedure, or the difficulty and personal expense of incorporating new curricular elements. According to Arends and Arends (1978), university faculty members are encouraged to act in autonomous and individual ways. In addition, faculty members outside the field of special education typically are not knowledgeable about exceptional children and do not view services to exceptional children as their concern (Drew and Perry, 1978). The combined effect of these factors has resulted in more resistance to change than project personnel had anticipated.

Another problem in legitimizing or institutionalizing change is the governance structure of teacher education programs. Traditionally, schools of education, along with their representatives in various governing organizations, have maintained a controlling influence over training programs (Fishell and Fox, 1976; Lucas, 1978). However, this situation is currently changing; many educational groups are struggling for control over teacher education in the areas of accreditation, certification, field experiences, and inservice education. D. G. Imig, the director of state and federal relations for the American Association of Colleges for Teacher Education, succinctly stated the issue of control: "Today, we are confronted with innumerable challenges to this control. We are confronted by a variety of 'communities' operating at the local, state, and national levels arguing that they are the legitimate constituencies of teacher education and should be the ones to set policy" (1976, pp. 2-3). We suggest that one of the reasons for this state of affairs is that there is little relevant evidence regarding the issue of who should govern, since little is known about what constitutes effective teaching and what conditions foster good teaching. Since there are various constituencies interested in teacher education, Lucas (1978) has proposed that the governance of teacher education programs should be reformed to provide substantial representation of all participants involved in the total process of education.

Within the university, the issue of governance also must be considered in attempts to change curriculum. Teacher education programs are literally brought into being by committees, kept in existence by committees, and ruled by committees (Ryan, 1980). Thus, they represent a compromise of many views and sometimes many political factors. Change in a setting such as this requires consideration of attitudinal change and other factors that perhaps would not be considered, for example, in a military or business setting (Drew and Perry, 1978).

In addition, most institutions of higher education have very few channels of communication between administrative units and very ineffective procedures for group problem solving (Arends and Arends, 1978). Thus, the means by which those who develop new programs can get the participation of groups that must implement their decisions are very limited. Therefore, institutionalization of change becomes not only extremely difficult but time consuming.

Corrigan (1978, p. 21) has written that "teacher education does not operate on a governance structure that allows it to control its own program development and reward system." Thus, the parameters of possible change are limited by such factors as university requirements, requirements of approving agencies, and other internal and external units or agencies influencing the design and operation of teacher education programs (Gilberts and Weisenstein, 1978). Smith (1980, p. 3) reviewed studies about reform in teacher education encompassing the past fifty years and concluded that these studies "overlooked the university arrangements that throughout the current century stunted the development of professional schools of pedagogy." However, he indicated that universities were not the only agencies "impeding the rise of genuine professional schools of education." He noted that accrediting agencies, teacher organizations, and various levels of government contributed to the chaos of the times. "In the entangling network of federal, state, and local agencies and private and professional groups, the actual political and social forces shaping pedagogical education are no longer obvious."

Overall, in regard to legitimization of new teacher curricula, there appears to be little evidence of widespread institutional curricular change. Where curricular change has been effected, there has been too little time to test the permanence or benefit of implemented change. Although curricular change and reorganization are considered to be the initial objectives of the Dean's Grants, most projects have illustrated what many change experts have predicted—change takes time. Hall (1978) indicates that change is a process, not an event; therefore, individual change must precede institutional change.

Evaluation. In addressing the issue of evaluation of curriculum, proponents of change in teacher education again had to address the existing problems in the teacher education curriculum. One of the major evaluation problems faced by those involved in effecting curriculum change has been the absence of a solid data base on which to compare teacher education programs before and after the intervention of a Dean's Grant. Consequently, the effectiveness of such interventions has been difficult to determine. Grotelueschen and Lahti (1978), speaking of evaluative practice in teacher education, indicated that evaluation has often been left to individual professors or departments and has often consisted only of questionnaires completed by students. Systematic and thorough curriculum evaluation has been difficult to achieve.

Not only have we tried to legitimize practices that have been initiated without a solid data base, but we in teacher education have assumed a reactive rather than a proactive posture in research and evaluation (Drew and Buchanan, 1979). An example specific to special education and teacher education is Scriven's (1976) warning against the inclusion of a test of positive attitude in evaluation of teacher training programs until overwhelming evidence is available that mainstreaming is better than previous practices. Scriven notes that public education is launching a switch to a concept that will be very expensive and may do children no good because we have done a poor job of evaluating the benefits of mainstreaming.

One of the few studies that has been conducted regarding the accomplishments of the Dean's Grant projects was exploratory in nature and was conducted with projects in the southeastern part of the United States (Hall and others, 1978). This study indicates that projects, for the most part, have focused on creating awareness of mainstreaming and building knowledge rather than on implementing and institutionalizing a new curriculum. In addition, there appeared to be little indication of movement on the part of faculty members (who were not already doing so) to include content regarding exceptional children in their courses, even though the project directors were functioning in a highly effective fashion.

While the activities of the Dean's Grant programs and other such endeavors have not found solutions to the more generic problems associated with teacher education curricula, addressing the process of curricular change has forced recognition of the problems associated with the structure of teacher education and the business-as-usual philosophy apparent in many programs. In all probability, the resources available to address the generic problems of teacher education have influenced the way and the degree to which extensive change was attempted. Some projects have attempted to overhaul the entire structure of teacher education, while others simply added courses or tracks to the already existing structure. Thus, the changes that were accomplished as a result of these projects are as varied as the number of projects. However, apparent changes or results fostered by the projects include the following:

1. A variety of strategies have been developed or employed to reorder or modify existing teacher education curricula.
2. A vast number of competencies have been identified for teachers who work with exceptional children.
3. A proposed curriculum structure has been developed for teacher education based on the provisions of P.L. 94-142.
4. A number of modules and other instructional materials have been developed that are directed toward helping regular classroom teachers gain competence in teaching exceptional children.
5. An awareness of the intricacies of and the need for change in teacher education has been established.

A Curriculum Model

In the foregoing section we have briefly discussed what we see as some of the conditions facing education technique, especially as they relate to preparing regular classroom teachers to teach exceptional children and to curriculum change. In the final section we will describe our recommendations regarding the teacher education curriculum. Our recommendations will be in terms of outlining a curriculum model.

We will discuss three major characteristics: governance of teacher education, the design of the curriculum, and evaluation. The issues of time, recruitment of students, selection of faculty, specific course content, and modes of instruction will not be considered. We believe that such issues need to be and can be addressed later.

Governance. We choose to discuss governance first, since our review of various teacher education criteria indicated a lack of plans for governance. We make the assumption that curriculum change will not occur within an organization unless curriculum planners understand the structure and process of governance, which is involved in the legitimization of the proposed changes. Imig (1976, p. 2) defined governance as "both structure and process. It has to do with authority to direct or control a function, a party, or a process. It is a structure legitimizing power-group relationships. It is a process for making basic decisions about purpose, procedure, and performance." We define teacher education as a program of study that prepares people to enter teaching. Included under the umbrella of a teacher education program are the various teaching fields: early childhood, middle school/junior high, English, math, science, and music. These teaching fields represent the areas of specialization within the teacher education program.

The basic unit of governance for a teacher education program should be the faculty members who teach the professional education courses. This program faculty should be empowered to initiate and/or review recommendations and proposals related to requirements for admission, curriculum, and degrees in teacher education. Furthermore, the program faculty should be given the responsibility for implementing and evaluating the curriculum. The chief administrative officer of the program should be the dean (or his or her delegate, who would serve as the director of teacher education).

Since teacher education involves a number of different constituencies, there should be a body that represents constituencies other than the program faculty. We recommend the formation of an advisory committee to the teacher education program faculty. This committee should at least include representatives from the schools of arts and sciences and education; public school administrators (principals and superintendents); and classroom teachers representing elementary, middle/junior high, and senior high schools. The advisory committee should be given the responsibility of reviewing and providing input on present and proposed curriculum and program policies.

For instance, the consideration of P.L. 94-142 by a teacher education program might result in the development of curriculum recommendations by the program faculty regarding the preparation needed by classroom teachers in the area of exceptionality. Specifically, the faculty might do the following:

1. Determine the skills, knowledge, and attitudes needed by teachers who teach exceptional children.
2. Review the existing curriculum to determine if any of the proposed skills, knowledge, and attitudes exist in the curriculum.
3. After reviewing the curriculum, determine how to best integrate the needed knowledge, skills, and attitudes into the existing curriculum.
4. By a specified time, submit in writing the faculty's recommendations to the dean.

Once a proposal or a recommendation has been approved by the program faculty, the dean of the program would submit the proposal to the faculty senate of the school, college, or department of education. The faculty senate includes representatives from all programs, including the teacher education program. The faculty senate should be empowered to review all curriculum or program proposals and to render judgment on the proposals. If the faculty senate approves the proposal or recommendation, the dean would then submit it to the appropriate administrative board of the university for final approval. The administrative board's responsibilities include, among others, the examining and approving of all proposed major curriculum changes. If the administrative board approves the proposal or recommendation, it then becomes policy. Figure 1 summarizes the structure and process of institutionalizing curriculum and program changes.

Design of the Curriculum. We are making the assumption that the purpose of a teacher education curriculum is the preparation of teachers who can bring about desired changes in pupils' performances and attitudes and who contribute to the ongoing development of the teaching profession. Additionally, the curriculum should be designed to allow for experimentation that, hopefully, will result in the development of prototypic models of curriculum. In conceptualizing our design we have drawn upon the ideas of James Earl Russell, the first dean of Teacher's College, Columbia University, and Lawrence A. Cremin, the present president of Teacher's College, Columbia University. In the 1890s, Russell laid the groundwork for professional schools of education. He believed that the curriculum should consist of four major components: general culture, special scholarship, professional knowledge, and technical skills. General culture referred to a basic foundation in the humanities, arts, sciences, and languages. Special scholarship was the concentration by a student in a particular discipline that he or she was preparing to teach. Professional knowledge related to the knowledge from the social sciences (especially psychology) that enabled a student to understand the nature of

Figure 1. Curriculum Development

```
┌─────────────────────┐         ┌─────────────────────┐
│ Teacher Education   │ ─ ─ ─ ─ │ Teacher Education   │
│ Advisory Committee  │         │ Program Faculty     │
└─────────────────────┘         └─────────────────────┘
                                          │
                                          ▼
                                ┌─────────────────────┐
                                │  Faculty Senate     │
                                └─────────────────────┘
                                          │
                                          ▼
                                ┌─────────────────────┐
                                │ Administrative Board│
                                └─────────────────────┘
```

schooling and learning. Russell defined technical skill as the component in which students would apply their knowledge and skill in actual teaching situations under the supervision of exemplary teachers (Cremin, 1978; Rugg, 1952).

Cremin (1978) further refined Russell's ideas about teacher education. Specifically, he addressed the components of professional knowledge and technical skills and combined them into professional studies. Professional studies included policy, developmental, and pedagogical studies. A further explanation of professional studies will be provided later.

Utilizing the ideas of Russell and Cremin, we propose a curriculum that is divided into three major components, as illustrated in Figure 2.

The first component, general studies, exists for all students in undergraduate programs at a university. It is designed to provide students with a broad background in English composition, foreign languages, mathematical sciences, the social sciences, the natural and physical sciences, the humanities, and fine arts. During the period of general studies, students develop a foundation in the disciplines necessary to areas of specialization and professional studies. The second component is specialization in which students develop

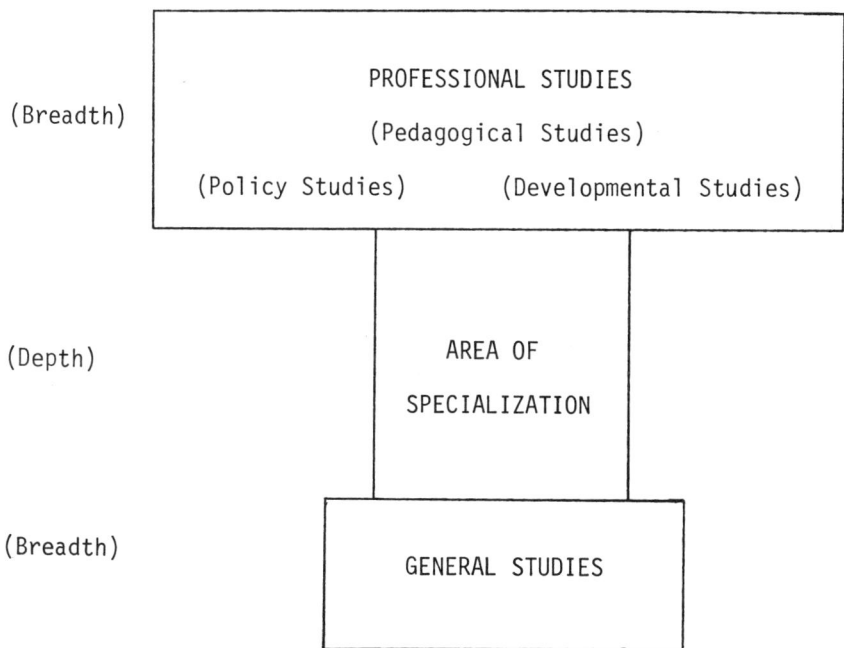

Figure 2. Components of the Curriculum in the Teacher Education Program

depth in a particular area of interest. This may be related to a discipline or the study of an age group such as early childhood. Areas of specialization constitute the teaching fields within a teacher education program. The first two areas, general studies and specialization, are similar to those components found in most liberal arts education. It is the third area, professional studies, where the student deviates from the basic liberal arts program and develops the breadth of knowledge and skills required for entry into the teaching profession. This component comprises three groups of studies: policy studies, developmental studies, and pedagogical studies. We have borrowed from Cremin's (1978, pp. 10-11) conceptualizations of policy studies and developmental studies. He defines policy studies as "those studies of the humanities and social sciences that contribute to an understanding of the aims of education and the situations and institutions in which educational institutions and the societies that sustain them are in turn affected by them." He defines developmental studies as "those studies of the humanities and behavioral sciences (including biology) that contribute to an understanding of human development over the life cycle and of various ways in which different forms of education affect that development. Of critical importance would be studies of socialization, acculturation, and learning to clarify the natural outcomes of the educational process." Pedagogical studies are defined as those studies that contribute to a teacher's understanding of and skill in curriculum planning and design, instructional methodologies, and evaluation. The pedagogical studies are mostly field-based, while the developmental and policy studies are campus-based and preclinical in nature.

Evaluation. Evaluation is a process for improving the curriculum and the quality of teacher education graduates. Through evaluation, faculty have data on which to base decisions regarding changes in the teacher eduation program. Since the late 1960s, teacher educators have been faced with several major questions. For example, why should institutions of higher education continue to spend resources to prepare additional teachers when a teacher surplus apparently exists? Why are pupil achievement scores declining?

Through a teacher education evaluation plan, a data base is established to provide information about the curriculum, students who enter and graduate from the program, and the later teaching experiences of the students. We suggest that there are five major components to the plan. The first step is to gather data about entering students. The second component collects information through specified research and evaluation projects. These projects are related to specific teaching fields, components of the curriculum, or an experimental project. The third step collects data from consumers, such as public schools and communities. The fourth component studies employment opportunities, and the final component gathers data from the teaching profession regarding such issues as the nature of the profession and the preparation of teachers.

We believe that an evaluation plan should be longitudinal in nature. Such a study should provide faculty and others with answers to the following questions: Who enters a teacher education program? What types of students are attracted to specific teaching fields? What areas of the curriculum need improvement? Do student attitudes change as a result of being involved in a teacher education program? Are there certain types of organizational climates within public elementary and secondary education that are more conducive to teachers? Who teaches? Do the graduates of a teacher education program influence pupil achievement? Who stays in teaching? A longitudinal study should provide the faculty and others with the possibility of comparing program results across the years (Burke, 1978).

References

A Common Body of Practice for Teachers: The Challenge of P. L. 94-142 to Teacher Education. Washington, D.C.: American Association of Colleges for Teacher Education, 1980.

Arends, R. I., and Arends, J. H. "Process of Change in Educational Setting: An Application to Mainstreaming." In J. K. Grosenick and M. C. Reynolds (Eds.), *Teacher Education: Renegotiating Roles for Mainstreaming.* Minneapolis: National Support Systems Project, 1978.

Behrens, T. R. Foreword to *A Common Body of Practice for Teachers: The Challenge of P.L. 94-142 to Teacher Education.* Washington, D.C.: American Association of Colleges of Teacher Education, 1980.

Behrens, T. R., and Grosenick, J. K. "Dean's Grant Projects: Supporting Innovations in Teacher Education Programs." In J. K. Grosenick and M. C. Reynolds (Eds.), *Teacher Education: Renegotiating Roles for Mainstreaming.* Minneapolis: National Support Systems Project, 1978.

Burdin, J. L., and Lanzillotti, K. (Eds.). *A Reader's Guide to the Comprehensive Models for Preparing Elementary Teachers.* Washington, D.C.: American Association of Colleges for Teacher Education, 1969.

Burke, W. I. "Teacher Education Study: A Research Preview." *Newsletter,* 1978, *63,* 11-13.

Conant, J. B. *The Education of American Teachers.* New York: McGraw-Hill, 1963.

Corrigan, D. C. "P.L. 94-142: A Matter of Human Rights—A Call for Change in Schools and Colleges of Education." In J. K. Grosenick and M. C. Reynolds (Eds.), *Teacher Education: Renegotiating Roles for Mainstreaming.* Minneapolis: National Support Systems Project, 1978.

Cremin, L. A. "The Education of the Educating Professions." *Proceedings of the 30th Annual Meeting of the American Association of Colleges for Teacher Education,* 1978, *1,* 5-24.

Denemark, G., Morsink, C. V., and Thomas, C. C. "Accepting the Challenge in Teaching." In *A Common Body of Practice for Teachers: The Challenge of P.L. 94-142 to Teacher Education.* Washington, D.C.: American Association of Colleges of Teacher Education, 1980.

Drew, C. J., and Buchanan, M. L. "Research on Teacher Education: Status and Need." *Teacher Education and Special Education,* 1979, *2,* 50-55.

Drew, C. J., and Perry, M. L. "Promoting Curricular Change in a College of Education." In J. K. Grosenick and M. C. Reynolds (Eds.), *Teacher Education: Renegotiating Roles for Mainstreaming.* Minneapolis: National Support Systems Project, 1978.

Eurich, A. C. "The 'Breakthrough' in Teacher Education." *The High School Journal,* 1960, *43,* 154-157.

Fishell, K. N., and Fox, W. L. "Facilitating Mainstreaming in Preservice and Inservice Programs in Higher Education." In P. H. Mann (Ed.), *Shared Responsibility for Handicapped Students.* Miami: University of Miami Training and Technical Assistance Center, 1976.

Gilberts, R. S., and Weisenstein, G. R. "Curriculum Change and Institutional Reorganization." In J. K. Grosenick and M. C. Reynolds (Eds.), *Teacher Education: Renegotiating Roles for Mainstreaming.* Minneapolis: National Support Systems Project, 1978.

Grotelueschen, T. S., and Lahti, L. I. "Perspectives on Evaluation." In J. K. Grosenick and M. C. Reynolds (Eds.), *Teacher Education: Renegotiating Roles for Mainstreaming.* Minneapolis: National Support Systems Project, 1978.

Hall, G. E. "Facilitating Institutional Change Using the Individual as the Frame of Reference." In J. K. Grosenick and M. C. Reynolds (Eds.), *Teacher Education: Renegotiating Roles for Mainstreaming.* Minneapolis: National Support Systems Project, 1978.

Hall, G. E., Loucks, S., George, A., Sharp, B., Schmid, R., and Lawrence, J. *An Exploratory Study of Implementation of Dean's Grant Projects in the Southeast.* Minneapolis: National Support Systems Project, 1978.

Hirst, P. H. *Knowledge and the Curriculum.* London: Routledge & Kegan Paul, 1974.

Howsam, R. B., Corrigan, D. C., Denemark, G., and Nash, R. J. *Educating a Profession.* Washington, D.C.: American Association of Colleges for Teacher Education, 1976.

Imig, D. G. *Nagging and Persistent Problems in American Teacher Education.* Washington, D.C.: American Association of Colleges for Teacher Education, 1976.

Iriarte, A. U. "Teacher Education Preparation Programs: A Commitment to Change." *Education Unlimited,* 1980, *2,* 22-24.

Lucas, C. J. "Teacher Education and Its Governance." *Educational Forum,* 1978, *42,* 469-482.

Martin, E. "Integration of the Handicapped Child into Regular Schools." *Minnesota Education,* 1976, *2,* 5-8.

Meyer, E. L. "Mainstreaming Colleges of Education." *Teacher Education and Special Education,* 1979, *2* (2), 5-8.

Rader, B. T. "Competencies for Mainstreaming Teachers: An Analysis." In J. K. Grosenick and M. C. Reynolds (Eds.), *Teacher Education: Renegotiating Roles for Mainstreaming.* Minneapolis: National Support Systems Project, 1978.

Reynolds, M. C. "Basic Issues in Restructuring Teacher Education." *Journal of Teacher Education,* 1978a, *29,* 25-29.

Reynolds, M. C. "Some Final Notes." In J. K. Grosenick and M. C. Reynolds (Eds.), *Teacher Education: Renegotiating Roles for Mainstreaming.* Minneapolis: National Support Systems Project, 1978b.

Rugg, H. *The Teacher of Teachers.* New York: Harper & Row, 1952.

Ryan, K. "Mainstreaming and Teacher Education: The Last Straw." In *A Common Body of Practice for Teachers: The Challenge of P.L. 94-142 to Teacher Education.* Washington, D.C.: American Assocation of Colleges for Teacher Education, 1980.

Saylor, J. G., Alexander, W. M., and Lewis, A. J. *Curriculum Planning for Better Teaching and Learning.* New York: Holt, Rinehart and Winston, 1981.

Scriven, M. "Some Issues in the Logic and Ethics of Mainstreaming." *Minnesota Education,* 1976, *2,* 61-67.

Smith, B. O. *Teachers for the Real World.* Washington, D.C.: American Association of Colleges for Teacher Education, 1969.

Smith, B. O. *A Design for a School of Pedagogy.* Washington, D.C.: U.S. Government Printing Office, 1980.

Stedman, D. J. "Possible Effects of P.L. 94-142 on the Future of Teacher Education." In *A Common Body of Practice for Teachers: The Challenge of P.L. 94-142 to Teacher Education.* Washington, D.C.: American Association of Colleges for Teacher Education, 1980.

Turnbull, A. P., and Strickland, B. "Successive Approximation: An Alternative Approach." In J. K. Grosenick and M. C. Reynolds (Eds.), *Teacher Education: Renegotiating Roles for Mainstreaming.* Minneapolis: National Support Systems Project, 1978.

West, T. L., and Bates, P. "Anatomy of a Dean's Grant Project." In J. K. Grosenick and M. C. Reynolds (Eds.), *Teacher Education: Renegotiating Roles for Mainstreaming.* Minneapolis: National Support Systems Project, 1978.

William I. Burke is the director of teacher education and an associate professor at the University of North Carolina at Chapel Hill.

Bonnie Strickland is a doctoral candidate and research associate in special education at the University of North Carolina at Chapel Hill. From 1976 to 1980, she served as the training coordinator for the Dean's Grant at the university.

Planning decisions regarding the field of special education have implications for trainers, employers, and monitors of personnel. This chapter describes a statewide cooperative planning approach for these groups.

The North Carolina Cooperative Planning Consortium: A New Approach to Planning for Special Education Manpower Requirements

Cathy L. Crossland
Linda P. Blanton

In the field of special education, unlike many other areas of teacher education, there is a legislative mandate requiring states to establish administrative structures to ensure that a sufficient number of trained personnel are available to render services in specific geographical areas and that such personnel have the technical skills to deliver appropriate services to students with special education needs. Such a mandate presents a great advantage to those who are responsible for implementing federal and state legislation pertaining to the education of exceptional students. It clarifies the legislative intent, that is, services are to be delivered according to a certain standard to a defined population with special needs. It also makes clear that it is the state education agency that is responsible for implementing the planning process. However, the legislation does not clearly indicate how, and by what administrative organization or procedure, the planning function is to be accomplished. There is the implication that the planning process must involve a partnership among a wide array of groups that share an interest in the general problem of manpower training and employment in the field of special education; the structure that will create this partnership is a matter left to the discretion of the individual states. Thus, the problem becomes not only one of establishing structures for planning but also one involving multiple groups for the purpose of developing partnerships and collaborative efforts.

State education agencies differ considerably in their interest in and capability of coordinating a cooperative planning effort. Comprehensive manpower planning requires the consideration of a range of substantive issues and administrative arrangements that have a greater breadth than is usually found within the purview of these state agencies. The types of organization, agencies, and interest groups that play important roles in the field of special education are those that *train* professional personnel (the universities and colleges that have schools or departments of education with curricula in special education), those that *monitor* the practice of teaching and the training of teachers (state education agencies and other agencies that credential personnel and review and approve training programs for certification), and those that *employ* teachers in the public and private sectors for direct service delivery (local education agencies and categorical service agencies), and those that seek to *influence* education policy and program development (professional organizations, labor unions, and lay special-interest groups with a focus on children with special needs). Understandably, state education agencies may not see the role as coordinator of planning for both the *production* and *deployment* of professional personnel in special education as either feasible or desirable. Moreover, few models for the implementation of coordinated planning have been tested and described.

Federal Efforts to Stimulate the Development of Cooperative Planning for Special Education

In an effort to provide useful models for the implementation of cooperative planning at the statewide level, the Bureau of Education for the Handicapped (BEH) sought to provide technical assistance to the states through the Project of Cooperative Manpower Planning in Special Education. Despite the fact that the legislation that mandated the planning function left the decision regarding the administrative structure for this purpose to the discretion of the states, the federal government gave the subtle impression that a unified or comprehensive planning model would be most appropriate. At least three important documents published during the formative period for state planning structures made this point of view clear.

First, the technical assistance manual prepared by the Project on Cooperative Manpower Planning in Special Education (Schofer and McGough, 1977) presents two organizational structures for accomplishing cooperative planning: (1) the centralized planning and program structure (single committee) model, and (2) the dual planning and program structure (one committee planning for manpower training and personnel development; one committee planning for classroom teacher requirements). In this manual, the strengths and weaknesses of the dual planning and program structure are discussed in great detail, while only the strengths of centralized planning and program structure are discussed.

Second, Schofer (1977, p. 22) reported at the second annual regional conference conducted by the Division of Personnel Preparation, a BEH organization, that: "It does not seem efficient for a state to have two committees that focus on the same thing: manpower planning, personnel development, and teacher training concerns. . . . If . . . persons within a state education agency are communicating and working together, and if college and university people are involved, then these matters may be meshed into a workable whole for one committee."

Third, in reporting the results of the second status study on statewide manpower planning, Schofer and Duncan (1978, p. 4) proposed that: "Developing and maintaining two committees within a state, both dealing with manpower planning, personnel development, and teacher training concerns is an unnecessary duplication of services. This duplication would be avoided if the individuals administering P.L. 94-142 within a state education agency would communicate, work together, and involve college and university people and others in forming a single committee."

Thus, the federal government spokesmen within BEH were clearly giving the impression that a unified planning structure involving trainers, monitors, and employers was the intent of federal legislation. As an indication of how states perceived a single committee approach as preferable, Schofer and Duncan (1978) reported that forty-two of fifty-three states or territories responding to a survey of planning efforts indicated that they had established single statewide manpower planning committees with comprehensive responsibilities for the implementation of the planning mandate.

The fact that so many states reported approaching the planning function with roughly the same organizational strategy does not mean that such strategies have been demonstrated to be more effective than multicommittee structures. Furthermore, we do not have sufficient information available to describe precisely the kind of planning process that has taken place in any of these states. To know that most states have only one planning body tells us nothing about the process or product of the planning endeavor.

This chapter is intended as a first effort to document the experience of a single state in the implementation of a cooperative planning committee approach to facilitate the manpower planning capabilities of institutions of higher education in the field of special education. In North Carolina, a structure has evolved to facilitate the planning process that has made it possible to deal with a range of issues and concerns of basic significance to the implementation of state and federal legislation pertaining to the assurance of educational opportunity for exceptional students. In this chapter, a description is offered of this model or strategy.

The Genesis of the North Carolina Cooperative Planning Consortium of Special Education Training Programs

Much of what has happened in North Carolina has emerged from a historical context that includes cooperative planning endeavors in the field of special education and antedating the enactment of P.L. 94-142. Moreover, the North Carolina experience has taken place in large part because there is a single structure for public institutions of higher education in the state. The organization of the sixteen campuses of the University of North Carolina (UNC) under a single administrative structure and the centralized budgeting for higher education have been important factors in the history and the success of the North Carolina planning process.

In early 1974, a group responsible for the administration of special education teacher training programs in North Carolina met to discuss the problems group members faced in making decisions about the size, scope, and direction of their respective educational programs. In addition, there was a recognized need to develop professional working relationships with one another. The outgrowth of these discussions was the formation of an informal network of persons who had a vested interest in special education teacher training programs across the state. This "consortium" arrangement was similar to many loosely formed confederations of professional peers—it had no funding base and no specific function. Rather, it emerged out of the need for a forum for the regular interchange of ideas about common problems.

In the fall of 1974, the Legislative Study Commission on Children with Special Needs (of the North Carolina General Assembly) requested the president of the UNC system to review the university's current education and training activities in the area of exceptional children and recommend the steps and resources needed to effectively expand and improve statewide service program development. The initial concern of this commission was related to unfilled teacher allotments in the state.

The already developing Cooperative Planning Consortium of Special Education Training Programs was designated by the UNC president to provide the university's response to the commission. The Advisory Budget Commission and the governor authorized the use of university-generated overhead receipts to support the consortium's effort. By virtue of these two decisions, a specific function for the consortium was identified and a funding base for its activities was established.

The UNC president assigned a second task to the consortium by requesting a long-range (five-year) plan that would address new directions and training program strategies designed to solve the problems involved in preparing enough well-trained professionals to work in the field of special education in North Carolina.

The membership of the consortium during its first year of operation was limited to representatives from those components of the UNC system with active training programs in the areas of special education, school psychology, and speech and hearing sciences. Additional members represented university campuses where programs were in the planning stage. This arrangement limited the membership to representatives from seven of the UNC public universities.

The efforts of the consortium during that initial year produced the first data-based review of existing teacher training programs in special education undertaken in North Carolina. This review culminated in the construction of a manpower training plan and a statement of the resources required to implement the plan within the state. Also, these activities clearly demonstrated the need for the consortium to exist on an organized basis as an advisory board to the UNC president regarding matters of university training programs in the special education field.

The consortium membership was expanded during the second year to include a chancellor-appointed representative from each of thirteen UNC campuses where programs to train personnel to work with children with special needs were either operational or in the planning stages. In addition, the eight private colleges and universities having similar programs were asked to caucus and elect a representative to the consortium so that the relevant private institutions would be represented in consortium activities and planning.

It had also become evident that decisions and prospective planning about manpower matters could not be made without a forum including those who *employ* and *train* special education personnel as well as those who *monitor* teacher training and classroom practice. Hence, representatives were added from the State Department of Public Instruction's Division for Exceptional Children, the Office for Children in the State Department of Human Resources, the North Carolina Association for Educators, the North Carolina Community College System, and the special-interest group called Parents and Professionals for Handicapped Children. This nineteen-member consortium, augmented by a staff of five part-time persons, constituted the new organizational format. The expanded membership was seen as an improvement from the first year, since it offered representation from all types of training programs from each of the major constituent campuses and organizations. In addition, it allowed the consortium to deal with geographical as well as organizational considerations without losing sight of the needs of special-interest groups, specialized disciplines, and professional organizations.

The current organizational model for the consortium evolved three years after its first meeting. At that time, it was determined that a more precise system for governing the group was highly desirable and a governance document was developed and approved by the membership. The role and function of the consortium was defined and the organizational tie with the general administration of the UNC system clarified in the governance document. Two representatives were added to the clearly specified membership — one from the North Carolina Department of Correction and one from the general administration of the UNC system. The method of election of officers, officers' duties, and meeting times were specified. Finally, standing committees were designated and a policy was established regarding special projects. The governance document provided a necessary structure in which the consortium could undertake its tasks and monitor itself. It facilitated the activities of the group by requiring that the chairperson of the consortium cannot serve more than two consecutive one-year terms, thereby disallowing the possibility that any one institution or person could dominate the organization.

The governance document also identified the linkage between the consortium and the federally mandated Comprehensive System for Personnel Development (CSPD) in North Carolina. The chairperson of the consortium serves as a member of the CSPD and in that capacity represents the institutions of higher education on that board. This clarification at an early stage of the interaction of these two groups averted what could have been a politically sensitive issue over the matter of duplicative manpower planning activities. The consortium acts as the advisory board to the university system in all matters related to manpower planning in the field of special education, while CSPD advises the state education agency on manpower planning requirements. The organizational relationship between the consortium and CSPD has strengthened both groups and enabled each of them to work more effectively within the state.

One of the essential operational characteristics of the consortium is its regularly scheduled meetings. These meetings are held four times a year and attendance is high. The consortium meets on a different campus each time and this rotating-site concept provides members with opportunities to visit each of the public and private campuses; to meet the chancellors and presidents of the institutions; and to interact with deans, department heads, and faculty.

At least once a year, the consortium meets with the special legislative commissions of the General Assembly that deal with the development of legislation related to special populations. Faculty members in other areas of teacher education rarely have an opportunity to make their views known directly to those persons responsible for making the laws that affect their professions.

The consortium has become a well-known organization in the field of teacher education in North Carolina, and its advice and wisdom are often sought by individuals and groups in matters related to special education programming. Consortium reports and statements are accorded respect; consequently, the conscientious and caring membership views participation in the organization as a serious professional commitment to the field of special education and the state of North Carolina. The consortium develops its agenda from a variety of sources. These include requests for information from the president of the university system, requests for data from the many state agencies such as the Department of Public Instruction or the Department of Human Resources, and individual institutional requests for technical assistance in program development or faculty recruitment. The consistent strand of the consortium's agenda, however, involves the issue of manpower planning.

The Consortium Model in Practice: Agenda for Manpower Planning

The North Carolina planning experience clearly indicates that a cooperative planning consortium can serve a number of functions not normally managed easily by planning bodies. One of the most unsuspected characteristics of such a consortium is the degree of commonality in particular generic problems. The distinctive differences in perspective among those who train, employ, and monitor the performance of educational personnel give the impression of widely diverse priority issues and concerns. It has become clear that among all participants in the consortium effort, the two most salient concerns are those related to the *quality* of preparation of professional personnel (and their performance) and the *equity of access* to educational opportunity for career entry and continued professional development throughout the state. These two issues, quality and access, have become the principal rubrics under which the agenda for the work of the North Carolina Cooperative Planning Consortium has developed. Illustrations of the work of the consortium in each of these areas indicate the ways in which the unified planning approach works.

Considerations of Quality. At least three illustrations can be given of the manner in which the consortium has dealt with issues of quality. In the first place, there is the matter of licensure and certification of professional personnel. In North Carolina, certification of teachers is the responsibility of the state education agency (SEA). This function is performed through approval of the educational programs offered by institutions of higher education. If an institution's curriculum is not approved by the SEA, graduates of that curriculum may not obtain certification from the SEA as teachers in that specialty area. In North Carolina, the consortium has been seen by the SEA as a forum in which the criteria for program approval may be discussed and in which the application of these criteria may be discussed with institutions of higher education offering programs and curricula in the field of special education. Moreover, the agencies that hire teacher personnel can express their own views of the preservice curriculum in order to better prepare graduates for classroom role responsibilities. Through this process the institutions are not surprised by an ad hoc set of evaluative criteria at the time of their next program assessment; the local education agencies and other employers are not surprised to learn that there are significant gaps in the education of the graduates they may hire from recognized (approved) training programs; and the state education agency can be confident that its program assessments are referenced to the criteria considered important by both the trainers and the employers of teachers.

In the area of preservice teacher certification, the consortium collaborated with the State Department of Public Instruction to produce a set of teacher certification competencies for each area of special education certification and one for regular education teachers who serve exceptional children. These competencies are now used by the State Board of Education as one of the bases for university program approval and teacher certification. A second major effort in the area of preservice teacher training that illustrates the work of the consortium has been the addition of two new areas of special education teacher certification in the state—cross-categorical certification and certification for teachers of the severely handicapped. As teacher training institutions within the state foresaw the need for these types of teachers, they developed programs to provide the personnel training. The consortium represented the consensus of all teacher training institutions when it requested that the State Department of Public Instruction recognize these additional areas of certification. By using a group process such as the consortium, individual institutions were able to capitalize on the asset of peer review and approval in designing training programs that are recognized by the certifying agency.

Another aspect of the concern for quality concerns the inservice education of classroom teachers. As the preservice, on-campus degree programs at North Carolina's colleges and universities have developed and stabilized, growing attention has been focused on how to make ongoing education and training available to persons who may wish to improve their professional skills through advanced on-the-job training. The consortium is undertaking data-based reviews of how to set a mechanism in place that will address, on an interinstitutional basis, the developing need for working teachers to receive continued professional preparation. This constitutes a new dimension to the traditional teacher training programs and the consortium activities in the area of inservice training will be important contributions to the state of the art in the field of teacher education.

Considerations of Access. There are several important aspects in considering equal access to educational opportunities in a specialized field of professional practice. In the first place, there is the consideration of the availability of sound programs for the preservice preparation of classroom teachers who may choose a career in the field of special education. A public system of higher education has a mandate to ensure the accessibility (to a reasonable degree) of a broad range of educational opportunities for its citizens. The fourteen campuses of the UNC system, plus the eleven private institutions, that have some form of special education program are widely dispersed geographically in the state. The consortium has been concerned with the problem of ensuring that opportunities for study in this field do not become so concentrated in certain universities or colleges that citizens living in other areas of the state are effectively prevented from entering this field. This same consideration becomes more important and sensitive as one approaches the matter of graduate education. In this respect, the consortium has had to deal with developing the appropriate contextual support for educational programs at the graduate level. Discussions have balanced the need for providing opportunities for career development (through graduate education) with the strengths of the individual institution, thereby recommending those places where specific categorical (for example, visual impairment or hearing impairment) special education graduate programs should be developed.

There has been a significant growth in the number of education programs for special educators at both the public and private institutions since the inception of the consortium in 1974. At that time, only six of the public institutions in the UNC system were approved to offer degree programs at either the undergraduate or graduate level of training. There are currently fourteen constituent institutions of the University of North Carolina authorized by the Board of Governors to plan or operate programs to prepare personnel to work with children with special needs. When these programs are in place, there will be undergraduate and graduate special education degree programs available on the campuses of the public institutions in each of the eight educational regions of the state, thereby accomplishing one of the consortium's long-range objectives. When the consortium was first organized, there were seven private institutions of higher education that were approved to offer degrees in special education. By 1980, that number had expanded to include ten private institutions with approved degree or certification programs. This growth represents the effects of collaborative manpower planning, much of it sponsored under the auspices of the consortium. In the matter of access to training, the consortium has worked to promote the appropriate balance between preservice, inservice, and field-based educational opportunities in the state. In this way, the evolving need for substantive preparation of entry-level practitioners and the continuing need for skill development and professional growth are integrated with a concern for the real distribution of demand for special education personnel and the availability of personnel to meet these needs.

The Consortium Strategy

Although the specific context for this consortium may not exist in other states, there are certain generic principles that we believe have characterized the North Carolina effort and which should be applicable in most other states. These principles are presented with the hope that they might serve to increase the ability to generalize this experience and at the same time constitute a kind of synthesis of the model described here.

Emphasis on the Autonomy of Individual Consortium Members. In abstract terms, the consortium is based on the principle of boundary maintenance among participating members. Individual institutions and organizations retain local autonomy and control over their programs. There is no attempt to make the consortium a policy-making body, even though several participants in the consortium have policy-making/implementation responsibilities in certain areas.

Emphasis on the Interdependence of Actions by Consortium Members. It is well understood by all members of the consortium that, even though each is autonomous, the actions of any one organization affect the activities of the other members in significant ways. A new degree program developed in one area of the state seriously lessens the possibility of a similar degree program elsewhere. There is an emphasis on the exchange of information and the anticipation of second-order consequences of particular decisions.

Emphasis on the Neutrality of the Consortium as a Forum for Exchange. The consortium is a forum within which the contribution of all parties (trainers, employers, and monitors) to an issue helps to diffuse and neutralize the controversy surrounding that issue so that meaningful discussion can take place. The emphasis is on exchange of plans, ideas, and aspirations as well as the exchange of lessons learned from direct experience.

Emphasis on the Treatment of Common Problems. The consortium is oriented toward planning for future manpower needs. Planning for the production of professional manpower (in any field) is a complicated matter. Precise estimates of the number of personnel required to meet a given level of need are difficult, if not impossible, to develop. There are considerations related to the estimated number of students likely to request particular types of special education services; population projections of all school-age children; legal mandates to provide certain categories of educational services; estimates of the numbers of teachers to be trained by the universities and colleges and the estimates of turnover in the current supply of professionals; and the matter of geographic distribution of educational opportunities for professional development through preservice, inservice, and field-based learning. All of these factors require reliable data and standardized definitions of the variables involved. For this purpose, the consortium must engage in a continual interchange among its members regarding the best and most appropriate conceptual models for the planning process.

Summary and Conclusions

More than six years have gone by since the inception of the North Carolina Cooperative Planning Consortium. It has been a period unlike almost any other concentrated time period in the recent history of special education. These years have been characterized by landmark federal and state legislative enactments that have guaranteed public educational services to all handicapped children and thereby set in motion a new frontier for professional educators. The urgent need for more classroom teachers who are prepared to work with various kinds of handicapped children has required institutions of higher education to increase the productivity of their special education teacher training programs. In addition, new teacher training programs have been planned and implemented at the undergraduate and graduate levels across the state as the public and private institutions expanded their capacities to meet the increasing manpower needs of North Carolina. Some of the greatest accomplishments of the colleges and universities across the state are encapsulated in this six-year time frame as they developed the capability to address the burgeoning educational needs of exceptional children.

Manpower planning is usually a *systematic* but rarely a purely *scientific* enterprise; it is also a political enterprise. The judgment and wisdom that come from experience have an important role in planning. The hard data available for planning purposes are rarely adequate to support a thoroughly objective planning solution. The search for solutions is a process of suboptimization, compromise, and a random collection of experience from others who have already faced the same or similar problems. The North Carolina consortium provides this opportunity for shared learning and mutual adjustment of institutional and public policy related to special education. It is a model that does not require extremely formal means of coordination, although leadership is important. It is a model that requires a broad and comprehensive range of perspectives among participants. It can facilitate the consideration and resolution of complex and sensitive issues in a cooperative and nonbureaucratic manner. It is a model that should be considered in planning for educational manpower needs.

References

Schofer, R. C. "Cooperative Manpower Planning." In J. Smith (Ed.), *Personnel Preparation and P.L. 94-142: The Map, the Mission, and the Mandate.* Division of Personnel Preparation, Bureau of Education for the Handicapped, U.S. Office of Education, 1977.

Schofer, R. C., and Duncan, J. R. *Statewide Cooperative Manpower Planning in Special Education: A Second Status Study.* Columbia: University of Missouri–Columbia, Department of Special Education, September 1978.

Schofer, R. C., and McGough, R. L. *Statewide Cooperative Manpower Planning in Special Education: A Status Study.* Columbia: University of Missouri–Columbia, Department of Special Education, November 1976.

Schofer, R. C., and McGough, R. L. *Manpower Planning for Special Education: Planning Model and Alternatives.* Columbia: University of Missouri–Columbia, Department of Special Education, August 1977.

Cathy L. Crossland is associate professor and coordinator of the graduate program in special education, School of Education, North Carolina State University at Raleigh.

Linda P. Blanton is associate professor, College of Human Learning and Development, Appalachian State University.

This chapter describes the approach of one university program for developing a field-based training program. Some of the important issues associated with this philosophical and programmatic redirection of university training are discussed, including collaborative planning, faculty support, program evaluation, and practica.

Field-Based Degree Training in Special Education

Donald B. Bailey, Jr.
David L. Lillie
James L. Paul

Field-based education is becoming an increasingly important way for universities to meet the current need for professional education. This need is especially apparent in special education and will serve as the primary focus of this chapter. This chapter has two purposes: to describe field-based education and the forces that are contributing to its development and to describe the professional, academic, and organizational issues that have been addressed in the development of three field-based master's degree programs at the University of North Carolina at Chapel Hill. In this chapter we will share some experiences, tentative conclusions, and partially formed hypotheses.

The focus is on the development of field-based master's degree programs because of the extensive experience in this area at the University of North Carolina at Chapel Hill during the past two years. A degree program is only one among many possible approaches to field-based training. We are not suggesting that this strategy is the most appropriate one for all teacher training institutions. It is hoped that the analyses, strategies, and ideas will be useful to others similarly engaged in the formulation of field-based policies and the development of field-based programs.

Field-based education refers to education activities that exceed the traditional campus-based degree and/or certification-oriented programs. It may be divided into two categories: university-initiated and client-initiated.

University-initiated field-based education is a program or activity that the university develops and delivers in response to perceived and/or assessed needs in some constituent organization or region. A field-based master's degree program to meet the degree-oriented training and career needs of employed teachers is an example of a university-initiated program.

Client-initiated field-based education is a program or activity that the university develops or delivers in response to a specific request. The clients who request university assistance are usually organizations or agencies. The actual target of the university assistance may be either the organization or specified employees in the organization. An extension course on a specified topic requested by a school for its teachers is an example of a client-initiated program.

Field-based education is offered by various means, depending on the needs to be addressed, the resources available, and university and client preferences. Examples of possible approaches include a degree program, a series of courses leading to certification, extension courses, workshops, consultation, and materials designed or organized to meet individual needs.

The Increase in Field-Based Efforts

In recent years a number of factors have combined to cause administrators, policy makers, legislators, funding agencies, and universities to view systematic, ongoing field-based training programs as crucial to professional development and the provision of quality services to children and adults served by educational agencies. These factors include the development of new knowledge, changes in the sociopolitical context of education, and the size and stability of the educator work force.

Knowledge Development. What we know about children's learning characteristics, curriculum design and development, and instructional approaches has increased to the point where the professional training and knowledge base of teachers can become dated unless there is some systematic approach to retraining and updating skills. The same situation exists for administrators regarding their knowledge and skills in the management sciences. As program planning and budgeting procedures, program-evaluation technologies, organizational development approaches, and other leadership techniques change, it is important to provide ongoing training if educational organizations are to remain effective.

Changes in the Sociopolitical Context of Education. The needs of teachers and administrators must be addressed within the context of the current social and institutional demands being placed upon them. The role of the public school in society is changing and these changes create new needs for knowledge, training, and organizational support. For example, since schools now assume more responsibilities than in the past for the socialization of children, it is necessary for teachers to know more about social and emotional development. Parents have been granted a more direct role in the educational decision-making process, thereby creating the need for teachers, administrators, and other professionals who provide educational support services to know more about the needs of families, working with parents, and the laws and ethics pertinent to these interactions. Handicapped children now have a legally guaranteed right to be served in the least restrictive educational setting. This right creates a need for changes in the delivery of special education services, increased knowledge and skills for regular classroom teachers who work with handicapped children, and development of the attitudes and skills of regular and special educators that will facilitate interdisciplinary functioning. Perhaps more than any other factor in education, this very real need for well-trained personnel to provide an equal opportunity for education to all the nation's handicapped children has made field-based and inservice training a major priority of the Office of Special Education, as well as that of many state education agencies.

Size and Stability of the Educator Work Force. While estimates vary, it is generally recognized that a large majority of the teachers who will be in the classroom a decade from now are already there. The number of new teachers entering the profession each year accounts for a relatively small proportion of the total number currently teaching. Therefore, if training is to have a significant impact on eductional practices, it must be provided to teachers who are already in the classroom and other educators who are already at work in the field.

Field-Based Efforts at the University of North Carolina–Chapel Hill

Within the past five years, American education has been challenged to secure a better match between higher education and the needs of public school systems. That is, the training resources of colleges and universities, traditionally committed to the preparation of educators to enter the profession, have been refocused to meet the training needs of educators already employed in public schools and other educational organizations. Resources have also been committed to assist the organizations directly through consultation and technical assistance as well as through staff development and training activities.

During the late 1970s, the division of special education in the School of Education at the University of North Carolina–Chapel Hill made a commitment to provide inservice training and continuing education at off-campus locations in an effort to address some of the needs described above. This commitment was determined through joint planning efforts involving the faculty, the State Department of Public Instruction, and the general administration of the University of North Carolina (UNC).

After substantial planning, it was decided that the university would provide off-campus master's degree programs. This decision was based upon three considerations. First, an assessment of the inservice teaching needs of public school teachers in North Carolina indicated a need for degree-oriented training. Second, there was evidence that field-based master's degree programs have been received well in other states. Northern Illinois University compared four different mechanisms for the delivery of field-based education: one- and two-day institutes, individual courses, off-campus master's degree coursework, and off-campus master's degree programs with a concurrent practicum. Of these alternatives, it was found that the off-campus master's degree with a concurrent practicum received the strongest internal and external support from both higher education and public school personnel (Miller and others, 1979). Third, as a result of statewide planning, the general administration of UNC was interested in establishing additional master's degree programs in special education with the assistance of the division of special education at UNC–Chapel Hill. Consequently, three field-based degree programs were established. Each was designed in response to different needs and provides a unique orientation and service delivery system. A brief description of each of these programs follows.

Fayetteville Graduate Center. The Fayetteville Graduate Center master's degree program is located on the campus of Fayetteville State University, Fayetteville, North Carolina. Fayetteville State University is a constituent member of the sixteen-campus UNC system. Fayetteville is approximately seventy-five miles south of Chapel Hill and is the central urban area for several counties in that region. Fort Bragg, a large military training installation, is on the outskirsts of Fayetteville and covers nearly forty square miles. The area population is approximately 250,000, including Fort Bragg.

Murdoch Center. Murdoch Center, located in Butner, North Carolina, is one of four state training centers for the mentally retarded. Butner is approximately twenty-five miles north of Chapel Hill. This program serves a rural area, although the several state institutions in the Butner area have a relatively large concentration of professionals engaged in work with handicapped individuals. The program at Murdoch Center was initiated at the request of the center's director and is designed to develop competencies for teaching and working with severely and profoundly handicapped individuals.

Elizabeth City Graduate Center. Elizabeth City is located in the predominantly rural northeastern corner of the state and is approximately 200 miles from Chapel Hill. The graduate center is located on the campus of Elizabeth City State University, a constituent member of the UNC system. This program leads to graduate certification in learning disabilities and mental retardation.

Issues in Field-Based Programming

The realignment of the training needs of public educational institutions with the technical and professional resources of the UNC system has involved complex organizational adjustments. It has been necessary to address a wide range of issues and questions not often raised by on-campus degree programs. These issues focus on administration, students, admissions criteria, faculty involvement, program content, and program evaluation. The remainder of this chapter will be devoted to a discussion of these issues and a description of some initial strategies that have been developed to resolve them. Given the fledgling status of these programs, it should be made clear that there are many unanswered questions. A discussion of issues and potential alternatives should be helpful, however, for other universities considering the field-based degree option.

Administrative Issues

Mutual Benefit. The major administrative issues encountered in offering a field-based degree program have emerged from the fact that the values and missions of two different kinds of organizations must be reconciled. The mission of the university is different from that of the public school system. If these two organizations are to work together toward effective field-based training, extensive collaborative efforts are required.

In order for two organizations to work together cooperatively and successfully, it is essential that both perceive and experience benefit from the effort. The primary benefit of field-based training for the public schools may be, for example, a more competent staff. The primary benefit for a school of education may be the assurance that it is providing a relevant program for which state resources will be made available on a continuing basis. For both the public school system and the university, the primary value is organizational stability. Stability is defined in terms of competent staff and relevant missions that are intellectually, financially, and politically supportable.

Co-Op, Not Co-Opt. Planning must occur in a way that assures all parties that mutually acceptable and desirable goals will be agreed upon and met. One of the most important influences that must be overcome in the planning process is the trust barrier. This problem goes beyond concerns about the competence of one organization to deliver or the ability of an organization to use professional resources. In many instances, it involves a fear of co-option. The university may be concerned about its training mission being co-opted by staff development units within public schools. Public schools may be concerned about inservice training and staff development resources being co-opted by universities to provide expensive training that may or may not be of practical benefit.

These issues and concerns are frequently unstated but they are present. They are dealt with by a process in which each party learns that the other party wants only what they say they want, and that they will deliver what they say they will deliver. The involved parties learn that they can depend upon each other to commit and use time responsibly and to deliver at an acceptable level of quality. If this does not occur, a productive relationship does not develop.

In order for an effective cooperative plan to be developed and implemented, the structure for planning must be clear. It must set the cooperating parties at ease by specifying how the interests of each party will be protected and how authority, as well as responsibility, will be shared.

Necessary Conditions for Development. There are two elements that we have found to be essential to planning. First, the heads of the organizations participating in cooperative planning must be directly involved and must give specific endorsement to the plan. Although the dean of a school of education and the superintendent of a public school system may not necessarily be involved in the detailed planning, each needs to make clear early his or her endorsement of the process and expectation of a product. Also, each must be involved in approving the developed plan.

Second, a written memorandum of understanding is needed. The memorandum of understanding should indicate who will do what and when they will do it. All matters related to the allocation and use of resources should be clearly specified. This involves agreements to share staff time or to make space available as well as budgetary considerations. The memorandum of understanding should specify the manner in which the program will be evaluated, who will evaluate it, when, and how. It should be clear from the agreement what would constitute success in the program and what would constitute failure. Accountability and the authority structure of the program should be clearly indicated, including who will make decisions about the training curriculum, who teaches what, who schedules training, who attends training sessions, who employs staff if staff must be employed, and so forth.

By setting forth such decisions in a written statement, the memorandum of agreement serves to prevent or reduce problems that may arise in the future. For example, such a memorandum allows the leadership in an organization to change without seriously affecting the cooperative program, since mutual expectations, benefits, and responsibilities have been set forth ahead of time.

Agreeing to develop a memorandum of agreement prevents organizations from starting a program prematurely. A good working relationship is a necessary condition to begin a cooperative program, but it must be complemented by an understanding of the specific terms for the program. Anticipation of a memorandum of agreement forces the organization to pay careful attention to the planning of the cooperative program. To sign a memorandum of understanding causes all parties to read the agreement carefully and take their obligations seriously.

Drafts of this agreement are useful to the coordinator of planning in each organization as an instrument for obtaining input from relevant individuals and groups within the organization. The final document is an important instrument for communication to boards, committees, or other official entities that need to be informed.

Finally, a memorandum of agreement provides (for the record) a basis for evaluating the program. Goals and intentions tend to become obscured over time. Therefore, it is important to have a written record of the initial purpose to guide the program and help answer the question of whether the goals are being met. It is always possible to change the goals, but it is important to be specific in those changes and to have a clear point of departure in discussions of program changes.

Program Development and Funding. Financing field-based education poses a major administrative problem. While requesting organizations often receive funds to contract with a provider organization for training, the time limits on the availability of these funds pose major problems for the agency desiring to provide the training. For example, in order for the university to deliver appropriate training, it must deploy faculty with the specific skills needed. Sometimes new faculty must be recruited. Job descriptions must be written, the university must approve a new faculty position, and a faculty member must then be recruited through appropriate affirmative action procedures. The training curriculum must also be developed. The curriculum and the programmatic structure for the delivery of the curriculum must be approved by the university, and this requires additional time. As a general rule, it is unrealistic to expect a university to discuss an appropriate training program, respond to needs identified in the field, and implement the program in less than a year.

It is important to distinguish between short-term and long-term commitments. Long-term training commitments involve more careful planning.

In a situation in which there is only one objective (for example, to offer a workshop on behavior management), planning is relatively simple and involves mostly logistical issues. A commitment to develop a field-based degree program, however, is a long-term commitment in which organizational policies and financial arrangements need to be considered and, in many instances, changed.

Investment in Planning. There are many start-up costs in developing a field-based degree program. Some of the start-up costs involve the planning process itself. While some of these costs involve the direct outlay of money, such as in the hiring of new staff or the purchase of supplies, much of the cost of planning is borne by the involved organizations in the form of existing staff time. Many staff members in both the receiving and providing agencies must give willingly of their time to attend meetings and be involved in planning and development activities. Unless there is a commitment to plan and implement the program under consideration, these resources may not be used effectively and barriers to the planning process can become insurmountable.

There is a tendency to underestimate the amount of time and resources needed to plan a long-term, cooperative, interinstitutional program such as a field-based degree program. As previously indicated, institutional policies may need to be changed to develop such a program. The institutional machinery for review and sanction is often complex. One organization's normal process of review and decision making is another organization's bureaucratic red tape.

Trust and credibility are important throughout the program development process. In the field-based master's programs described earlier, for example, review by the following university organizations or individuals was required: the special education division faculty, the executive committee of the school of education, the administrative board of the graduate school, the chancellor of the university, and the president of the university. There had to be agreement within the university among the coordinator of field-based programs within the division of special education, the division chairperson, the associate dean for field-based services in the school of education, the associate dean for academic affairs in the school of education, the dean of the school of education, and the dean of the graduate school. All parties had to be informed about all proposals and had to share some understanding of and commitment to the process by which the program would be developed.

There are hundreds of hours invested by professionals in the process of informing and being informed and making reasonable decisions about the program. What is described here is only the review within the university. The cooperating school or institutional system had its own process of review in the examples described earlier. In the planning process, it is important that the principal parties help one another understand the other's home institution—how it works and the process by which approval is obtained. There is no substitute for frequent, honest communication, such as giving a progress report on the review and approval process.

Students

The potential students of a field-based degree program will affect many decisions regarding the program, including admissions criteria, course content, and course scheduling. For example, there may be many basic concepts that need no introduction to experienced teachers. But, if field-based students have been out of school longer than on-campus students, then a refresher course to update basic concepts may be necessary.

During the planning of the field-based degree programs at UNC it was assumed that some characteristics of the students enrolling in field-based programs would be different from those of students enrolling in on-campus programs. After two and a half years of administering and implementing field-based master's programs, we have found some characteristics of the two groups to be quite different. Table 1 illustrates several characteristics of field-based students as compared to campus-based students.

As can be seen in Table 1, field-based students, on the average, are approximately four years older than on-campus students. The range in age is much broader for field-based students, and approximately 20 percent of all field-based students are over age thirty-five, as opposed to approximately 4 percent of on-campus students. On-campus students have less teaching experience prior to entrance into the training program than do their field-based counterparts. The proportion of male and female students is approximately the same in both programs.

Table 1. Characteristics of Students Enrolled in Field-Based and Campus Master's Degree Programs

		Age		Sex		Years Teaching Experience	
	N	Mean	Range	Male	Female	Mean	Range
Field-based[a]	49	30.2	21–50	10%	90%	4.4	0–19
Campus[b]	26	26.3	21–36	10%	90%	1.9	0–14

[a]1979–1981
[b]1980–1981

These data have a number of implications. For example, it appears that a field-based program may reach an older population of teachers who ordinarily may not have the opportunity to return to graduate school due to financial or family considerations. Also, differences in the teaching experience of field-based and on-campus students may have some bearing on the content and organization of training. For example, more than 98 percent of all field-based students enter the program with paid teaching experience, as compared with only 55 percent of all on-campus students.

Admissions Criteria

The issue of admissions criteria for students in field-based degree programs raises a number of interesting questions and often places the program between two groups with competing priorities. Public education agencies would like as many staff members (students) as possible to take advantage of the program. More staff members (students) per course means more training per dollar. In some cases, school administrators may observe teachers who are in serious need of extensive training and may strongly encourage them to consider pursuing further education. This raises the question of whether a field-based graduate program should serve as a remedial training program for poor or mediocre teachers or as an opportunity for outstanding teachers to further develop their skills and thus become "master" teachers.

University faculty would like to ensure that on-campus standards of quality are not compromised by field-based programs. The reputation of the university, its training programs, and its faculty is invested in the program. This viewpoint suggests that admissions criteria for students in the field-based programs be the same for those as for students entering on-campus programs. This issue may be partially resolved by an examination of the purpose of a field-based system. When such a program is a degree program, it would seem that the broad purpose should be similar to that of on-campus programs. To the extent that this is true, field-based degree programs should incorporate admissions criteria that are similar to on-campus requirements.

Since the purposes of our programs are very similar, the UNC field-based programs have used the same admissions criteria that have been used on campus. These criteria include a minimum grade point average, completion of the Graduate Record Examination (GRE) at an acceptable level, and three strong letters of recommendation. We believe that this was a wise decision, since some university faculty and review committees believe that off-campus coursework is less rigorous and of a lower quality than on-campus coursework. Consequently, establishing different criteria for off-campus admissions would probably have resulted in a lack of support and approval for the programs.

A significant issue has developed around the acceptable level of GRE scores. Table 2 compares the GRE scores and undergraduate grade point averages of field-based students and on-campus students. As may be seen, the field-based students did not fare as well as on-campus students when taking the GRE. Although the grade point average of field-based students is also lower, the discrepancy is not as great as that found in GRE scores.

There are a number of possible explanations for this discrepancy in GRE scores. The GRE measures general academic knowledge and there may be a recency-of-academic-experience effect. That is, the more recently an individual has been involved in a formal and prolonged academic experience (that is, undergraduate training), the higher she or he may score on the GRE. As indicated in Table 1, on the average, field-based students have been away from a formal academic experience much longer than on-campus students. Another possibility is that teachers who are capable and confident in their ability to perform on tests like the GRE decide earlier to apply for on-campus enrollment, leaving those teachers who are less capable and confident in their academic ability to wait for the availability of field-based programs in hopes that such programs will be easier to enter.

If field-based programs are to expand, the use of the GRE as a screening device needs to be examined. The literature in this area is confusing. Jones and Ezzell (1979) recently reported only a very slight relationship between GRE scores and subsequent graduate school grades, particularly in professional schools. Of perhaps more importance, a meaningful positive correlation between GRE scores and teaching competency in special education has yet to be found (Lillie, 1979). However, university faculty will continue to judge the quality of graduate programs by the quality of GRE scores of the entering students. If field-based programs are to flourish, a careful examination of the usefulness of this and other criteria will have to be conducted.

Table 2. Comparison of GRE Scores and Undergraduate GPA of Students Enrolled in Field-Based and Campus Master's Degree Programs

	GRE			GPA		
	N	Mean	Range	N	Mean	Range
Field-based[a]	49	905	640–1160	49	3.14	2.2–3.9
Campus[b]	26	993	700–1340	22	3.44	2.6–4.0

[a]1979–1981
[b]1980–1981

One alternative to traditional approaches to admissions is to incorporate on-campus standards but also to examine other factors as predictors of academic success. For example, a large number of students applying for admission to our field-based programs have already taken several graduate-level courses, primarily through various extension programs or through courses in other field-based programs. Successful performance in these graduate-level courses may be used as one predictor of success in the graduate program, when this information is available.

Faculty

Faculty participation and support is a critical element of a successful field-based educational program. During the planning stages of the field-based program at UNC–Chapel Hill, it was decided that as one means of quality control at least 50 percent of all coursework offered in each field-based master's degree program must be taught by full-time, on-campus faculty. If the program is to be seen by the students, the community, and other faculty as a legitimate extension of the campus program, the utilization of faculty who are identified with the on-campus program is necessary. Acceptance of an off-campus program greatly depends on the assumption that the quality of the program does not vary from campus to the field-based site. This policy has been very important in establishing faculty acceptance of our program. Faculty are aware of the competencies of their on-campus colleagues. Acceptance of off-campus programs will therefore improve as the knowledge of or perception of the competency level of the utilized faculty improves.

One important factor leading to the successful implementation of the field-based master's degree program offered by UNC–Chapel Hill has been the establishment of a full-time, on-site faculty position. When the Fayetteville Graduate Center program was implemented, a faculty member was recruited and placed in Fayetteville. Fortunately, this faculty member was a recent graduate of the doctoral program at UNC–Chapel Hill and therefore was very aware of the scope and sequence of the master's degree program. The on-site faculty member teaches approximately two courses a semester in the field-based program and is also responsible for the counseling of the master's degree students who are enrolled. The local coordination, communication, and daily personal contact with students has proved to be a valuable asset to the success of the program. The practice of locating a full-time faculty member at the site proved to be so important in the Fayetteville program that it was decided that this approach would also be used at the other two field-based master's degree sites.

Motivation for Faculty Participation. There are a number of issues revolving around the participation of on-campus faculty in continuing field-based programs. The following chart lists several reasons faculty may have for participating in such activities as well as several reasons why faculty members may not want to participate:

Reasons for Participating	*Reasons Against Participating*
1. A personal philosophy that a school of education must meet the training needs of the public schools	1. Promotion and tenure criteria do not recognize the importance of teaching, particularly off-campus teaching
2. A belief that inservice teachers are realistic and stimulating	2. It is time-consuming and takes away from time to undertake research or other scholarly activities
3. Enjoyment in having continuous contact with the "grass roots" of education	3. Colleagues see it as a low status activity
4. A feeling that a real need is being met	4. It is seen as "extra" work with inadequate extra salary
5. A belief that more can be learned about the issues and problems in education than is the case when teaching on-campus	5. Competition with private consulting work that is already being undertaken by faculty members with greater compensation
6. Supplemental salary can be earned	

One of the biggest detriments to faculty involvement in field-based education deals with promotion and tenure. At a large state research university such as UNC–Chapel Hill, a primary consideration for promotion and tenure is scholarly productivity. As a result, junior faculty members may not necessarily see field work as promoting their career development. This disadvantage for participating in field-based coursework has been offset somewhat by the capability of earning supplementary salary at a time when faculty salaries are not keeping up with inflation. The long-term solution to this problem requires consensus by all faculty that field-based efforts are indeed a part of the mission of a school of education and that each faculty person has some responsibility to field-based programs.

Program Delivery

The content of most on-campus degree programs is determined by a number of factors, including departmental orientation, school-wide goals, demands in the world of work, and priorities of individual faculty members who teach the courses that comprise the program. Program content is affected to a large extent by the fact that graduating students will be faced with a wide range of possible career options. The pressure to ensure that most students will be successful in a number of related jobs may force many programs to provide a broader-based content than would otherwise be the case. State certification packages may have the same effect. For example, in North Carolina certification in mental retardation entitles one to teach any level of retardation from kindergarten through twelfth grade.

Although these variables also contribute to decisions regarding the content of field-based degree programs, the fact that most participants are already employed in a specific job adds an additional dimension for consideration. This dimension affects a number of decisions about the program; the major ones are the scope and sequence of the coursework, the nature of practicum experiences, and ways of packaging courses. The issue of broad-based training, which prepares students for a variety of work options, versus more specific training in response to the needs of students and their employing organizations affects curriculum decisions.

Content. Decisions regarding the array of coursework provided to field-based students include number, content, and sequence. At first glance, it might appear that the number of courses in a field-based program should be the same as the on-campus program; however, the unique features of a field-based effort may indicate otherwise. Field-based students have fewer opportunities to interact with faculty outside of class time, to do independent readings and research, or to make use of other university resources such as libraries, test files, ongoing research projects, diagnostic clinics, or model intervention programs. In recognition of this difference in access to resources outside of class, the field-based degree programs at UNC require more coursework than do the on-campus programs (thirty on-campus semester hours versus thirty-six field-based semester hours). The goal is to compensate for low accessibility by bringing the information to students in the form of coursework.

The content of field-based courses, in many instances, does not vary significantly from that of on-campus courses. Again, however, there are dimensions of field-based programs that may call for flexibility in this area. For example, the on-campus UNC program requires a course that teaches the details of writing Individual Education Plans (IEPs). If a school system has completed a year-long series of inservice training sessions on the IEP, the necessity of repeating the information in a field-based course is questioned. Likewise, we question the need to teach behavior management principles to students who are employed at a residential institution for the severely retarded where systematic application of learning principles has been emphasized consistently through inservice training and close supervision.

In many cases, decisions regarding what to teach can be accomplished by conducting a thorough needs assessment at the beginning of each course. Students who can pass a competency exam may not be required to take the course at all. If a large majority of class members are already skilled in a certain area, then perhaps that area can be eliminated from the course and other relevant topics substituted. Class members who do not know the material can be assigned specific readings or other outside activities.

Another issue regarding program content is the flexibility that is offered to students to supplement their degree program with electives or independent studies designed to meet individual training needs. The very nature of field-based efforts limits this type of program flexibility. Administrative and financial concerns that dictate necessary course enrollments make it economically impractical to offer a wide variety of program alternatives. Limited faculty time and limited access to adequate library resources serve to restrict the possibility of independent study as an alternative solution.

In consideration of these issues and limitations, a number of strategies have been incorporated in our field-based efforts. First, the entire course sequence of the field-based programs is composed of required courses. Although this limits the options for some students, the coursework provided (in addition to the extra six hours in the field-based program) is usually sufficient to meet the broad needs of most students. Second, some course requirements may be waived for students who demonstrate certain competencies.

Although the credit-hour requirement is not waived in this case, students have the option of taking another course with the approval of an advisor, either on our campus or at another university offering graduate-level coursework. Third, in conjunction with this strategy, we have expanded from six to twelve the number of credits that may be transferred from another institution. This allows for some flexibility in coursework and does not penalize students who have built up a substantial number of graduate credits at other institutions. Also, it maintains the on-campus standard of a minimum of twenty-four hours being taken in the program.

Practica. Practica for on-campus students are designed to ensure that preservice teachers exhibit a certain level of competence in applying skills in intervention settings and to provide exposure to a range of teaching styles, handicapping conditions, and service-delivery systems. These goals are met by placing students in classrooms where master teachers provide an exceptional teaching model and give feedback to student teachers through daily supervision. This type of practicum experience is not usually an option for most students in field-based programs because they typically are already teaching in their own classrooms. However, there are some advantages to this arrangement. Teachers generally know their children quite well and are ready to begin refining skills without the usual "get-acquainted" period. Teachers have full control over their classrooms, thus avoiding the problem of convincing a cooperating teacher to try a new technique or gather a certain type of data.

The disadvantages, however, are readily apparent. Supervision is a major problem. Students are not working under the direction of a master teacher, and faculty members will have difficulty making frequent site visits, particularly if students are dispersed over a large geographical region. Full-time employment means that there will be little if any opportunity to work with a range of children. This arrangement may be appropriate if the teacher plans to continue working in a similar environment with similar children, but when certification allows teaching in significantly different environments, it becomes more difficult to justify such a limited internship experience. For example, North Carolina certification in mental retardation allows one to teach any level of retardation from kindergarten through twelfth grade. The extent to which a teacher of first grade EMH children should be exposed to programming for severely retarded adolescents and other similar issues must be addressed in determining the nature of field-based practica.

Given these limitations, adjustments were made in the UNC field-based curriculum that ensured adequate student training. One strategy we employed was to begin by individualizing the internship experience. Faculty members who were responsible for supervision made an initial site visit to determine strengths and weaknesses as exhibited in the current placement. Then a "contract" was drawn up between student and professor clearly delineating the skills to be developed as a part of the internship and outlining the activities to ensure that goals would be met and evaluation was possible. The internship was then used to refine existing skills, apply new teaching procedures, systematically gather data, and evaluate other dimensions such as room arrangement and scheduling. The lack of frequent supervision makes such a contract essential. Activities and goals are clearly specified as well as criteria for mastery. Progress is evaluated through permanent products, such as charted data, written instructional plans, assessment reports, and through interviews and site visits, when possible.

Although the exposure to a range of settings may be limited, there are appropriate experiences that can begin to meet this goal. For example, one approach to determining goals and objectives for children is to examine the requirements of each child's next most probable placement. Teaching these required skills increases the probability of successful placement. One appropriate internship activity is to have teachers identify future probable placements for their children and to conduct an assessment of the skills important for survival in those placements. Such an activity surely falls within the realm of teacher responsibilities and provides some exposure to other existing programs. The same sort of activity can also be conducted at the other end of the continuum. Teachers can be asked to view their own classrooms as future placement sites for some children and examine the skills essential for success in their own programs. Teachers may then evaluate other programs or classes to determine whether they are in fact adequately preparing children for this transition. Sharing this information with the programs whose children may enter the teacher's class not only improves services to children but also gives teachers an opportunity to observe a range of intervention settings.

Course Packaging. The unique characteristics of field-based degree programs require some alternatives to the way we currently package courses. Several factors militate against traditional packaging. Teaching is a strenuous and demanding occupation. Two days per week filled with teaching, driving to class, attending a three-hour class session, and driving home (in addition to outside reading requirements) add significantly to this stress. For field-based degree programs to be successful, the benefits of completing such a program must be clearly stated and must constitute sufficient reward to ensure continued participation. Although there are a number of positive outcomes of such a program, increased pay and improved marketability as a professional are probably the most powerful incentives. But even these may be insufficient when weighed against the sacrifices that must be made.

We are just beginning to investigate other strategies in terms of course packaging. The possibilities are numerous but have yet to be systematically evaluated. For example, instead of attending one three-hour evening class per week, perhaps students would prefer a lengthy Saturday session once a month. Programmed instruction using self-instructional packets, filmstrips, or even computer-assisted instruction are also alternatives worth investigating.

Evaluation

Given the developmental status of field-based degree programs, a comprehensive evaluation plan is critical from both a formative and summative perspective. Good evaluation data may be used to determine a program's strengths and weaknesses, demonstrate the effectiveness of the training to the public educational systems served by these programs, determine if students are satisfied and will continue with the program, and establish a firm empirical rationale for the continuation of field-based efforts.

The evaluation process consists of at least three broad steps. First, important goals or potential outcomes of the program must be identified. Second, techniques for measuring the extent to which each goal or outcome is accomplished must be determined and implemented. Finally, a decision must be made, on the basis of data gathered, whether or not the program was effective. Evaluation of field-based degree programs requires unique considerations in each of these steps.

In using such a model at the University of North Carolina, we have identified at least four broad evaluation concerns. The first concern addresses the impact of the program on the performance of duties in professional settings by the students. Certainly, one outcome of a field-based degree program should be a significant improvement in the performance of professional duties. As a result of completing the program, students should have improved their ability to accurately assess and evaluate their own students, design appropriate instructional programs, deliver instruction according to an instructional plan, conduct ongoing evaluation of the effectiveness of instruction, implement generalization strategies to ensure maintenance and functional use of new skills, and participate effectively in the interdisciplinary process. Initial evaluation efforts at UNC–Chapel Hill have included impact data of this type. One of the best ways to find out how well teachers are acquiring skills for performing in the classroom teaching situation is by direct observation. During the first two years of operation of the Fayetteville Graduate Center program, students were observed a number of times in their teaching situations and rated on the North Carolina Teacher Observation Scale (a locally developed observation scale). The scale offers an opportunity to rate students from one to five (1 = lowest, 5 = highest) across fifteen categories.

Affective Style
- Enthusiasm when working with children
- Confidence and poise in maintaining learning environment
- Patience and understanding toward children
- Teacher language behaviors

Instructional Abilities
- Responsibility in general classroom operations
- Ability to keep class attention on task
- Use of positive reinforcement
- Use of positive discipline procedures for decreasing inappropriate behaviors
- Skill in presenting material

Classroom Organization
- Sensitivity to the effects on learning of the physical conditions of the classroom
- Instructional organization
- Teaching toward generalization of concepts and operations

- Individualizing instruction within a group structure
- Selecting and using teaching materials
- Initiative and resourcefulness in curriculum planning.

Table 3 presents a comparison of the initial student rating with the final rating for the first six program graduates. In all instances, gains were made by the students between the initial and final ratings. The program is currently re-evaluating the observation and rating process for possible modification or use of another instrument.

The second broad evaluation concern addresses the impact of a field-based program on the attractiveness of a public institution to employees. An ongoing professional training program may make employment at a given institution a more attractive option for prospective employees and could serve to improve some aspects of personal perception of job satisfaction, such as feelings of competence, sense of control, meaningfulness of work, and so forth.

The third evaluation concern addresses staff satisfaction with the program from the perspective of both the student and the administrative staff. Successful implementation surely depends in part on the extent to which participants view it as meaningful, well organized, and fair. It is critical that the administrative staff of local educational agencies have sufficient and frequent opportunity to express their satisfaction with the organization, administration, and outcomes of the training program. Continued support of the program depends heavily on administrative approval of general aspects of the program, such as the admissions process, and that the program be perceived as relevant to the needs of the participants and the organization.

A satisfaction questionnaire has been used to gather indicator data in this area for the program offered at the Fayetteville Graduate Center. Table 4 is an example of the data collected in the summer of 1980 from approximately forty students enrolled in that field-based degree program.

Overall mean ratings in all categories fell between good and excellent on the scale, indicating general student satisfaction with the program.

Table 3. North Carolina Teacher Observation Scale Ratings for Graduates of the Special Education Program

Student	August 1980 Graduates Initial Rating	Final Rating
A	40	52
B	57	59
C	44	50
D	46	59
E	40	56
F	47	55

Table 4. Second-Year Student Satisfaction Questionnaire —
Fayetteville, Summer 1980

Questionnaire Categories	Overall Mean Ratings*	Range Sub-category Mean Ratings
Advising Procedures	4.38	4.26–4.50
Coursework/Content	4.16	4.03–4.30
Coursework/Instruction	4.23	3.97–4.47
Personal/Professional Development	4.32	4.17–4.46

*Scale Used	Unsatisfactory 1	Mediocre 2	Satisfactory 3	Good 4	Excellent 5

Finally, the fledgling status of most field-based degree programs mandates evaluation strategies designed to demonstrate that on-campus quality is maintained in off-campus degree programs. This is particularly critical in the situation where the field-based program is being implemented on an experimental basis. University faculty associated with the program, as well as those not directly associated, will be concerned with the broad range of program quality ranging from admissions criteria to course evaluation criteria.

Once evaluation data have been gathered, the information must be used to determine the extent to which the field-based program has met its stated goals. At least two criteria may be used to make such a decision. Minimum standards of competency in specified skill areas may be used as one criterion. For example, the evaluation advisory board may suggest that each graduate should be able to design an instructional program that contains all necessary information. Such a standard gives a clear criterion against which student performance may be evaluated. This is an appropriate strategy when standards of mastery are clearly agreed upon or can be clearly specified. Other evaluation measures may not be so clear and may require the use of a comparison group. Although expensive, gathering data on a comparison group may provide clear data that indicate program effectiveness or point out new directions for program growth or revision.

Field-based programs will not live or die on the basis of evaluation data alone. Politics and funding priorities will surely play a major role in this decision. However, for the present, the burden of proof falls on the program itself. Given the current lack of consensus as to the importance of field-based degree programs, it is essential that adequate evaluation designs be planned and implemented. Only through such an approach can we ensure high-quality programs and decide the future status of field-based degree efforts.

References

Jones, L. V., and Ezzell, C. *Prediction of First-Year Graduate Grades at UNC-CH with Emphasis on the GRE Analytical Test.* Chapel Hill: University of North Carolina at Chapel Hill, the L. L. Thurstone Psychometric Lab (No. 160), October 1979.

Lillie, D. L. *First Annual Report: The Fayetteville Field-Based Master's Degree Program in Special Education.* Chapel Hill: University of North Carolina at Chapel Hill, School of Education, June 1979.

Miller, S. R., Stonebrenner, R. L., and Miller, T. L. "Moving the University to the Student: A Model." *Educational Horizons,* Winter 1979.

Note: For an excellent review of field-based models, the reader is referred to Nelson, M. C. (Ed.). *Field-Based Teacher Training: Applications in Special Education.* Minneapolis: Advanced Training Institute, University of Minnesota, 1978.

Donald B. Bailey, Jr., is a clinical assistant professor in the School of Education, University of North Carolina at Chapel Hill, and coordinator of the field-based master's degree program at the Murdoch Center.

David L. Lillie is a professor in the School of Education, University of North Carolina at Chapel Hill, and coordinator of field-based programs in the Division of Special Education.

James L. Paul is a professor in the School of Education, University of North Carolina at Chapel Hill, and chairman of the Division of Special Education.

The authors review our current state of knowledge concerning the preparation of teachers for mainstreamed classrooms and make suggestions for future efforts.

Attitudes and Teacher Mainstreamed Classrooms: A Review of Research

Barbara H. Wasik
Rune J. Simeonsson

The Education for All Handicapped Children Act of 1975, P.L. 94-142, is a legislated mandate calling for the least restrictive alternative as a policy for guiding education decisions about handicapped children. As a result of this act, the placement of handicapped children into the regular classroom has become a frequently selected educational option. Unfortunately, the implementation of P.L. 94-142 has proceeded largely without information regarding the characteristics of an educational environment that are most facilitative for the academic success and emotional adjustment of handicapped children. This lack of research has serious legal as well as social consequences. To redress this situation, there is a need for systematic research examining the relationship between environmental variables and the achievement and adjustment of handicapped children.

The authors appreciate the helpful suggestions of Jill E. Fishbein and Heidi Shaw during the preparation of this chapter.

A model of behavior proposed by Albert Bandura (1977) could be used to investigate important relationships in the child's classroom environment, especially those relationships between the teacher and the child. Such investigations could yield important information for preparing teachers to work with handicapped children in the regular classroom.

Bandura states that a person's behavior at any time is a function of an interaction among the person's environment, personal factors (for example, attitudes), and the person's own behavior. To study the handicapped child's performance in the classroom, the schematic diagram shown in Figure 1 can be used to show interrelationships between the child and teacher. The child's behavior is a function of an interaction among the child's environment, the child himself, and the child's behavior. The teacher is a part of the child's environment and, as such, influences the child's behavior.

Figure 1. Interrelationships Between Child and Teacher

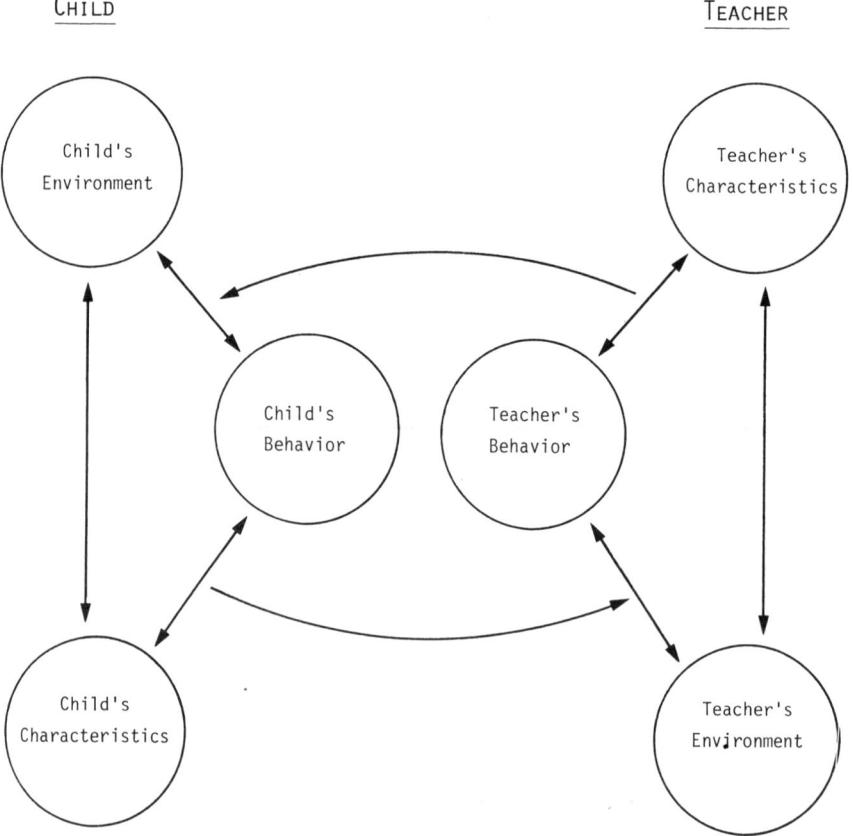

Teacher behavior is also influenced by the teacher's own characteristics and by the teacher's environment. Teachers come to the classroom setting with a set of attitudes, expectancies, and beliefs. These variables interact with teacher behavior, such as instructional procedures or child management skills, to affect child behavior but, since the child is part of the teacher's environment, the child also influences teacher behavior, and thus a reciprocal interaction results.

In this chapter, one aspect of this reciprocal interaction will be considered, specifically teacher attitudes. In a recent literature review, Alexander and Strain (1978) emphasized that the characteristics of the successful teacher of handicapped children include not only skills and competencies but attitudes as well. The opinionnaire data that Alexander and Strain reviewed indicated that regular classroom teachers, particularly those with limited special education training or experience, were unlikely to support mainstreaming of handicapped children. They also concluded that teachers assumed such children would generally benefit less from schooling. Alexander and Strain recommended that further research should address issues of teacher training with specific reference to the skills and strategies that teachers need to teach handicapped children within the regular classroom.

Some initial research has been conducted on such teacher variables, both preceding and following implementation of P.L. 94-142. This chapter will build on and extend Alexander and Strain's review in order to determine the implications and suggestions that can be made for teacher education programs and to identify gaps in knowledge that should be pursued in future research studies.

For the purposes of this chapter, teacher characteristics are limited to a study of attitudes, expectancies, and beliefs; attitudes will be considered the more generic term. From the review of research on teacher attitudes pertaining to exceptional children, three categories are used to organize the research: documentation of attitudes, identification of attitudinal correlates, and the modification of attitudes. While it is beyond the scope of this chapter to carry out a critical evaluation of research studies, a brief review of the findings will be made under each of the categories, followed by a synthesis of the findings.

Documentation of Attitudes

The nature of attitudes toward exceptional children has been investigated in a number of descriptive studies. In these studies, investigators have typically examined the attitudes of regular class teachers, although some studies have compared the attitudes of different school personnel. In a few instances, the attitudes of preservice students have been assessed as well. Vacc and Kirst (1977) assessed the attitudes of 102 regular class teachers toward either mainstreaming or special class placement of emotionally disturbed children. Their findings indicated that teachers favored the segregation of emotionally disturbed children into special classrooms and that teachers believed that emotionally disturbed children would not be accepted by their nonhandicapped peers. Furthermore, they concluded that teachers did not believe that mainstreaming would be beneficial for emotionally disturbed children and that these children would have a negative effect on the teacher's program in the classroom.

A study similar to that reported by Vacc and Kirst (1977) was conducted by Hirshoren and Burton (1979) with sixty-seven teachers at elementary and secondary levels. Teachers were presented with vignettes portraying children with five different handicapping conditions at five levels of severity. Findings indicated that regular teachers were more willing to assist in mainstreaming behavior disordered children than mentally retarded children regardless of severity. Children with sensory or physical handicaps were given an intermediate rating between the two.

In an attempt to assess receptiveness to a state law calling for integration of handicapped children, Wechsler and others (1975) carried out a survey of 639 teachers on attitudes toward different handicapping conditions of a physical nature in a middle-sized community in Massachusetts. Results from 86 percent of the teachers indicated that they felt that children with asthma, heart conditions, or crutches and braces would be more suitable for integration than children with visual, hearing, or seizure problems. They also found that teachers who had previous experience with physically handicapped children had more optimistic attitudes toward the children.

The role of teachers' previous experience with physically handicapped students was also investigated by Frith and Edwards (1981). A significantly greater concern about responsibilities pertaining to toileting, administering medication, and paperwork was expressed by teachers without experience teaching physically handicapped children than by teachers who had taught such children.

Guerin (1979) assessed the concerns of teachers regarding mainstreamed educably mentally retarded and educationally handicapped children (for example, learning disabled and emotionally disturbed). In response to questions on the degree of comfort or discomfort experienced with special children in a variety of situations, teachers indicated greater comfort with supervisory and academic responsibilities than those involving the child's social competence. Teachers also reported that they were less comfortable with retarded than educationally handicapped children. In another study carried out by Guerin and Czatlocky (1974), the attitudes of regular class and special class teachers were compared with those of administrators. In regard to attitudinal reactions to the integration of educably mentally retarded children, 94 percent of the administrators held a positive attitude toward integration. Sixty-two percent of the teachers were positive, 19 percent held neutral attitudes, and 19 percent had negative attitudes.

Moore and Fine (1978) compared the attitudes of teachers from regular classes with those from classes for educably mentally handicapped and learning disabled children. Teachers were asked to complete checklists for three hypothetical children: an educably mentally handicapped child, a learning disabled child, and a normal child. Findings indicated that teachers viewed the three child types differently. Furthermore, teachers of educably mentally handicapped and learning disabled were more accepting of mainstreaming such children than teachers of regular classes. All teachers were more in support of mainstreaming learning disabled children than educably mentally handicapped children.

In another comparative study, Boote (1976) compared the attitudes of 136 teachers and 50 principals drawn from randomly selected schools on the allocation of inservice time activities in special education. Significant differences were obtained between teachers and principals; principals desired less change than teachers. While a positive relationship was found between grade taught and overall satisfaction with the special education inservice program, years of experience and possession of a master's degree were found to be essentially unrelated to attitude. Pratt (1978) also studied differences among school staff. He compared the attitudes of principals, regular classroom teachers, special education teachers, and librarians toward placement of handicapped children in mainstreamed classes. The attitudes of teachers in a target school with an adapted program involving staff development activities were found to be more positive than those of teachers from comparison schools without such a program.

Few studies on the topic of attitude characteristics have focused on preservice student trainees. Buttery (1978) assessed the affective response of undergraduate teacher trainees in the areas of early childhood, elementary, and middle school to ten exceptionality types. Findings indicated more favorable responses to having one exceptional child than several in the regular classroom. Nash (1978) compared the knowledge of future teachers about exceptionality and types of handicap by examining differences on a knowledge inventory between students taking a survey course in special education and students in an educational psychology course. Findings indicated more overall knowledge about exceptional children and generally more knowledge in specific areas for students having special education training than those without exposure to the course.

Substantial variability characterizes the literature reviewed on attitudes of teachers toward handicapped children and special education. In spite of differences in the questions and the populations surveyed, some common trends seem evident. The findings of several studies indicate that the type and severity of handicapping conditions does influence acceptance; chronic illness is seen as more favorable than sensory impairments (Wechsler and others, 1975) and children with emotional or learning disorders are more accepted than retarded disorders (Guerin, 1979; Moore and Fine, 1978). Furthermore, one handicapped child is favored over several in the classroom (Buttery, 1978). There is also support for the fact that training and/or experience does contribute to more knowledgeable (Nash, 1978) and more accepting teachers (Moore and Fine, 1978; Pratt, 1978; Wechsler and others, 1975).

Identification of Attitudinal Correlates

For the second major area of research, studies have focused on attitudinal correlates of teachers concerning special children. One early study on attitudinal correlates was carried out by Proctor (1967). The attitudes and knowledge of regular class teachers, special education teachers, ancillary personnel, and student teachers were compared. Findings indicated that special education and ancillary personnel held more realistic attitudes than teachers with fewer academic courses pertaining to special children. It was also found that amount rather than type of teaching experience related to the achievement of realistic attitudes toward educational placement of special children.

In a study of attitudes on the acceptance of handicapped children into the classroom, Stevens and Braun (1980) assessed the responses of regular classroom teachers from the kindergarten through eighth grade. It was found that teachers in the primary and middle grades were more accepting of handicapped children than teachers of seventh and eighth graders. Furthermore, more favorable attitudes toward handicapped integration were associated with teachers who had more special education courses and held positive beliefs about the importance of handicapped children and the responsibility of public schools to educate such children. The chronological age and the sex of the teachers were, however, not correlated with positive attitudes.

Cline (1981) also found that attitudes of principals toward handicapped children were not differentiated on the basis of sex, experience with a program for handicapped students, or elementary versus secondary settings. However, principals with less than ten years of experience were more knowledgeable about special children than those with more than ten years of experience.

Peters (1977) compared the attitudes toward acceptance and knowledge of exceptional children by resource room and regular classroom teachers. The hypothesized association between type and amount of teaching and positive attitudes was not supported by the findings. No differences in attitudes of acceptance of exceptional children were found as a function of type and amount of teaching experience. Differences were found as a function of the number of academic credits that teachers held. The responses of forty regular classroom teachers were used to investigate the relationship of knowledge of teaching skills, teacher attitude, knowledge of placement, and the integration of handicapped/nonhandicapped by Carey (1978). The teachers used as a reference one handicapped and one nonhandicapped child in their classroom. Significant correlations were found among a number of variables, including attitude, knowledge of placement of handicapped children, skill knowledge, and corrective intervention. In general, teacher attitude and skill level were significantly associated with the categories of teacher-pupil interaction of the teacher with handicapped pupils.

DeLeo (1976) carried out a comprehensive survey of 2,300 school personnel, including directors of special education, special education teachers, principals, and regular teachers. The directors of special education held the most favorable attitudes toward integration of exceptional children. Special education teachers were next, followed by principals and regular teachers, who held the least favorable attitudes toward integration. Using the size of the community as a marker, medium and small communities were generally associated with more favorable views toward integration than large communities.

Research reviewed under the heading of attitudinal correlates, while limited, does reveal some common findings. As might be expected, more realistic and favorable attitudes toward handicapped children are associated with professional roles that involve such children (DeLeo, 1976; Peters, 1977; Proctor, 1967). While age and sex of teachers do not seem to be associated with favorable attitudes, teaching placement in elementary rather than high grades is a positive correlate.

Modification of Attitudes

The last section to be reviewed, which covers the modification of teacher attitudes, skills, and knowledge in relation to the education of handicapped children, is of potential importance for preservice and inservice training of teachers. Unfortunately, little systematic effort has been devoted to improving the attitudes of regular classroom teachers about working with handicapped children (Johnson and Cartwright, 1979). The meager amount of research in this area has limited the initiation of curriculum changes to make teacher education programs more effective (Burke and Strickland, 1981). A review of available research, however, may provide initial information about strategies and procedures of potential relevance for curricular development.

One of the earliest investigations of attitude modification of classroom teachers toward exceptional children was done by Haring (1957). The specific purpose was to modify teacher attitudes toward greater acceptance of exceptional children through the utilization of a workshop format. Workshops were provided for all regular classroom teachers from four schools, three of which were public and one was parochial. Pre- and post-testing was designed to assess change in knowledge regarding exceptional children, acceptance of such children, and personality characteristics of the teacher. A general conclusion was that the workshop format significantly increased the information and understanding that teachers had about exceptional children. Attitude change, however, was related to specific schools because teachers who became more accepting of exceptional children had a greater number of experiences with exceptional children in the classroom. Teachers from schools with fewer exceptional children in the classrooms showed no significant change in acceptance. In a second study, Glass and Meckler (1972) examined the effects of a summer workshop to prepare teachers to instruct handicapped children in the regular classroom. Eighteen regular class teachers were provided experience with thirty-eight exceptional children. The focus of the workshop was on changing attitudes and beliefs, improving diagnostic skills, teaching remediation, and enhancing interpersonal relationships skills. Teachers were given classroom teaching experiences, problem-solving sessions, formal instruction, feedback and planning sessions, and parent meeting opportunities. Results indicated that significant gains were made in the attitudes, beliefs, diagnostic skills, and remediation management abilities of teachers as a function of the experience as measured by a standardized attitude inventory and a self-report inventory.

Other studies have involved the comparison of a treatment group with a control or contrasting treatment group. Riggen (1978) carried out a study to evaluate the effects of inservice training with 300 elementary school and junior high teachers and principals from twenty-two schools. It was hypothesized that teachers who were provided with such training would show improved attitudes toward handicapped children and that such change should be associated with an initial level of high or low dogmatism. The findings indicated that inservice training clearly contributed to a more positive attitude change among teachers receiving such training than among control teachers. The hypothesized relationship between attitude change as a function of high or low dogmatism was not consistent.

In a second study involving experimental and control groups, Fisher (1975) compared the effect of a student training center program with a traditional program on the attitude and behavior characteristics of student teachers. The student teaching center program involved a sixteen-week period of on-site field experiences, whereas the traditional plan consisted of half of a semester of coursework and half a semester of field placement. Results indicated that the type of student teaching program was not reflected in differences of attitude toward handicapped children. Nevertheless, student teachers in the experimental program demonstrated higher scores on "humanistic" teaching behavior characteristics and significantly higher scores were recorded for the control group on "task-oriented, businesslike" teacher behavior. Although there were no changes in attitude, it does appear that specific behavior characteristics changed as a function of the teaching program. This is not surprising, because attitudinal changes often follow mastery of skills.

The impact on teacher attitudes of a resource room program to integrate handicapped children into regular classes was examined by Shotel and others (1972). A comparision of teachers in experimental schools and teachers in schools with self-contained classes revealed minimal effects on attitudes toward retarded and learning disabled children, although some positive effects were found toward emotionally disturbed children.

Singleton (1977) compared the two programs altering attitudes and expectancies of seventy-six regular elementary classroom teachers. Two inservice programs were compared with a control condition. One inservice program involved direct assistance with resource specialists and the second consisted of workshops covering various topics. It was found that the attitude scores of the control group and the direct-assistance group were higher than those of the workshop group. This finding pertained to a subscale of the dependent measure focusing specifically on learning disabled children. No differences were observed between groups as a function of a subscale on emotionally disturbed subjects. Additional comparisons were also made by dividing the direct-assistance group into classifications based on the presence or absence of handicapped classes at the school. It was concluded that the direct-assistance program was more effective in generating attitude change toward learning disabled children than emotionally disturbed children. Expectancies for educationally handicapped children were found to vary as a function of type of inservice training and presence or absence of special classes at the school.

Johnson and Cartwright (1979) studied the effects of information and experience on teacher's knowledge and attitudes about mainstreaming by gathering data on prospective regular classroom teachers. Data from three groups of prospective teachers were analyzed. One group was enrolled in both an information or content course and a course that focused on experience with exceptional children. The remaining two groups were enrolled in either the content course or experience course. No differences among the three groups were found on a post-test measure of knowledge. Teacher attitudes toward mainstreaming, however, improved when they had a combination of information about and experience with the handicapped; attitudes also improved for those who had the content-only course. The authors concluded that knowledge had a greater effect on attitudes than they had predicted.

Of the seven studies reviewed in this area, two earlier studies reflect attempts to document the effect of a specific intervention on a pre-post basis without reference to a control group. The other five studies do involve comparison groups in which differential intervention was provided to determine effects on attitudes and characteristics of teachers. While positive attitude and skill changes have been found as a result of pre-post testing of a group provided specific training, results have been less clear when obtained by research involving experimental and control contrast groups. In studies involving training of perspective teachers, Fisher (1975) found no differences in attitude toward handicapped children as a function of two types of programs, but Johnson and Cartwright (1979) found that attitude changes were obtained from participants in a knowledge course alone as well as a course combining knowledge and experience. Attitude effects of inservice experiences as well as experimental programs have been mixed. While the findings indicated favorable attitude change as a function of specific training experiences, these changes do not correlate with predicted personality constructs (Riggen, 1978) and were specific to certain types of handicapping conditions and/or training formats (Shotel and others, 1972; Singleton, 1977).

In conclusion, research on teacher attitudes pertaining to handicapped children does not provide a clear overall picture. In an earlier study, Mackie and others (1957) attemtped to determine the competencies needed by teachers of the emotionally disturbed and socially maladjusted child. They studied eighty-eight potential competencies by having teachers make ratings in terms of their proficiency on each area. Bullock and Whelan (1971) took this same list of competencies and asked a group of teachers of emotionally disturbed and socially maladjusted children to rank the items, again in terms of importance and proficiency. In general, the teachers in the second sample tended to rank the items similarly on importance and proficiency. Of more direct interest here are the implications drawn by Bullock and Whelan. They stated that "more intensive empirical research must be undertaken to determine the most important competencies needed by teachers of emotionally disturbed and socially maladjusted children. Without this research, teacher preparation institutions are lacking scientific data to substantiate their existing programs and to serve as guidelines for program development and expansion" (1971, p. 488).

The results of research over the last decade have not substantially moved the field forward in making it possible to specify recommendations for enhancing the role of the teacher in teaching the handicapped child in the classroom. One of the problems may be that both the procedures for identification of handicapped children and the measurement instruments used vary across studies. Although there is still some support for the conclusion of Alexander and Strain (1978) that regular class teachers in general do not favor integration of handicapped children, there is also support that positive attitudes do increase as a function of experience and training. Furthermore, specific interventions in the form of workshop and inservice programs seem to contribute to positive attitude change and improve behavior characteristics of teachers, even though the impact of such intervention is not consistent across studies. Taken as a whole, however, the studies do indicate that without exposure to the characteristics of handicapped children and without knowledge of their special needs, teachers are less likely to consider the educational needs of handicapped children than they would with such exposure. Additionally, while training to work with handicapped children in and of itself may not guarantee attitude change, it does appear to enhance teacher attitudes in the form of positive acceptance of and commitment to their educational needs.

References

Alexander, C., and Strain, P. S. "A Review of Educators' Attitudes Toward Handicapped Children and the Concept of Mainstreaming." *Psychology in the Schools*, 1978, *15*, 390-396.
Bandura, A. *Social Learning Theory*. Englewood Cliffs, N.J.: Prentice-Hall, 1977.
Boote, K. "Principal and Teacher Perceptions of Special Education Inservice Programs for Regular Elementary Teachers." *Dissertation Abstracts International*, 1976, *37* (1), 217-218a.
Bullock, L. M., and Whelan, R. J. "Competencies Needed by Teachers of the Emotionally Disturbed and Socially Maladjusted." *Exceptional Children*, 1971, *37*, 485-490.
Burke, W. I., and Strickland, B. "A Process for Curricular Change in Teacher Education." In D. J. Stedman and J. L. Paul (Eds.), *New Directions for Exceptional Children: Professional Preparation of Teachers of Exceptional Children*. San Francisco: Jossey-Bass, 1981.
Buttery, T. J. "Affective Response to Exceptional Children by Students Preparing to Be Teachers." *Perceptual and Motor Skills*, 1978, *46*, 288-290.
Carey, J. A. "The Interrelationship Between Teacher Skill Knowledge, Attitude Toward, Knowledge of, and Behavioral Interactions with Handicapped Children in the Regular Classroom." *Dissertation Abstracts International*, 1978, *39*, 6051.
Cline, R. "Principals' Attitudes and Knowledge About Handicapped Children." *Exceptional Children*, 1981, *48*, 172-174.
DeLeo, A. V. "The Attitude of Public School Administrators and Teachers Toward the Integration of Children with Special Needs Into Regular Education Programs." *Dissertation Abstracts International*, 1976, *37* (2), 915-916a.
Fisher, E. B. "An Evaluation of a Student Teaching Center Approach in Special Education to Developing Teacher Characteristics and Attitudes at Kean College of New Jersey." *Dissertation Abstracts International*, 1975, *36* (6A), 3563.
Frith, G. H., and Edwards, R. "Misconceptions of Regular Classroom Teachers About Physically Handicapped Students." *Exceptional Children*, 1981, *48*, 182-184.

Glass, R. M., and Meckler, R. S. "Preparing Elementary Teachers to Instruct Mildly Handicapped Children in Regular Classrooms: A Summer Workshop." *Exceptional Children,* 1972, *39,* 152–156.

Guerin, G. R. "Regular Teacher Concerns with Mainstreamed Learning Handicapped Children." *Psychology in the Schools,* 1979, *16,* 543–545.

Guerin, G. R., and Czatlocky, K. "Integration Programs for the Mildly Retarded." *Exceptional Children,* 1974, *41,* 173–179.

Haring, N. G. "A Study of Classroom Teachers' Attitudes Toward Exceptional Children." *Dissertation Abstracts,* 1957, *17,* 103–104.

Hirshoren, A., and Burton, T. "Willingness of Regular Teachers to Participate in Mainstreaming Handicapped Children." *Journal of Research and Development in Education,* 1979, *12* (4), 93–100.

Johnson, A. B., and Cartwright, C. A. "Roles of Information and Experience in Improving Teachers' Knowledge and Attitudes About Mainstreaming." *Journal of Special Education,* 1979, *13,* 453–462.

Mackie, K., and Williams, H. *Teachers of Handicapped Children Who Are Socially and Emotionally Handicapped.* Washington, D.C.: U.S. Government Printing Office, 1957.

Moore, J., and Fine, M. J. "Regular and Special Class Teachers' Perceptions of Normal and Exceptional Children and Their Attitudes Toward Mainstreaming." *Psychology in the Schools,* 1978, *15,* 253–259.

Nash, G. L. "A Comparison of Knowledge of Exceptional Children in Three Groups of Future Teachers at the University of Alabama." *Dissertation Abstracts International,* 1978, *39,* 2185.

Peters, R. S. "A Study of the Attitudes of Elementary Teachers Toward Exceptional Children in the Mainstream." *Dissertation Abstracts International,* 1977, *38,* 5396.

Pratt, S.E. "Attitudes of Educators Toward the Placement of Exceptional Children: A Comparative Study." *Dissertation Abstracts International,* 1978, *38,* 2040.

Proctor, D. I. "An Investigation of the Relationships Between Knowledge of Exceptional Children, Kind and Amount of Experience, and Attitudes Toward Their Classroom Integration." *Dissertation Abstracts,* 1967, *27,* 1721.

Riggen, T. F. "An Investigation of the Covariance of Dogmatism and Inservice Training on the Attitudes of Principals and Classroom Teachers Concerning the Mainstreaming of Mildly Handicapped Children." *Dissertation Abstracts International,* 1978, *38* (11A), 6454–6455.

Shotel, J. R., Iano, R. P., and McGettigan, J. F. "Teacher Attitudes Associated with the Integration of Handicapped Children." *Exceptional Children,* 1972, *38,* 677–683.

Singleton, K. "Creating Positive Attitudes and Expectancies of Regular Classroom Teachers Toward Mainstreaming Educationally Handicapped Children: A Comparison of Two Inservice Methods." *Dissertation Abstracts International,* 1977, *38* (1A), 186–187.

Stevens, T. M., and Braun, B. L. "Measures of Regular Classroom Teachers' Attitudes Toward Handicapped Children." *Exceptional Children,* 1980, *46,* 292–294.

Vacc, N., and Kirst, N. "Emotionally Disturbed Children and Regular Class Teachers." *The Elementary School Journal,* 1977, *77,* 309–317.

Wechsler, H., Surez, A. C., and McFadden, M. "Teachers' Attitudes Toward the Education of Physically Handicapped Children: Implications for the Implementation of Massachusetts Chapter 766." *Journal of Education,* 1975, *157,* 17–24.

Barbara H. Wasik is professor and associate dean in the School of Education at the University of North Carolina at Chapel Hill. She is also a researcher at the Frank Porter Graham Child Development Center.

Rune J. Simeonsson is professor in the School of Education at the University of North Carolina at Chapel Hill. He is also a researcher at the Frank Porter Graham Child Development Center.

*This chapter portrays society in transition from
an industrial to a communcations perspective; correspondingly
rapid and dramatic changes lead educators to find
new planning tools.*

Educating Special Teachers: Inventing the Future

*Paul F. Fendt
Marvin D. Wyne*

The purpose of this chapter is to examine the potential value of futurism as a relevant philosophy and strategy for improving current approaches to the education of special teachers and planning special teacher education in the years ahead. The aim here is not to read the collective palm of special education or make mystical predictions of impending wealth or doom. As Gallagher (1981, p. 264) astutely observed, "Future forecasts are made tolerable only by the poor memory of those who have listened to past predictions." While a debt to the ancient and compelling practice of oracles and seers must be acknowledged, futurism has evolved from an occult art in the direction of an applied science. Futurism has miles to go before reaching scientific maturity, but embryonic methodologies have emerged that can add an important tool to the practices of planning, evaluation, and long-term goal establishment. Futurism is long-range planning rather than short-range planning and has a number of synonyms (such as future studies).

This chapter looks first at teacher education and posits a disparity between teaching and instruction. Following a rationale for the application of futurism to the issue of special teacher education is a brief descriptive comparison of alternate approaches to future studies. The chapter culminates in the application of a technique of futurism called *futures invention* to the planning and evaluation of special teacher education.

Teachers and Teaching: State of the Art

The practice of teaching and the education of teachers have not changed in their essential form and substance over the past half century. It is true that the period of required preservice training has been extended from two years in the "normal school" to four years in the present "teacher's college" and, more recently, expectations for inservice education throughout the teaching career have risen markedly. The context of the teaching profession has surely been affected by such factors as collective bargaining, accountability, smaller classes, federal aid and its attendant guidelines, mandatory achievement testing, competency testing, a burgeoning layer of administrative bureaucracy, and mainstreaming. However, the state of the art of teaching and teacher education cannot be shown to have advanced commensurate with the growth of knowledge about school learning.

If the effectiveness of teaching can be validly judged on the basis of student performance, it can be charged that the state of the art of teaching, hence teacher education, has actually regressed during the past two decades. One searing statistic is only too well known—Scholastic Aptitude Test scores have declined each consecutive year since 1962. During that same period, the per pupil cost of education has increased each consecutive year, even in the face of declining pupil enrollment (Wirtz, 1977). The bill of indictment grows longer with evidence that the teaching profession is experiencing the toxic effects of cumulative mediocrity of teacher ability. An examination of teacher employment records and performance on the National Teacher Examination of more than 30,000 North Carolina teachers who entered the public schools between 1973 and 1980 indicates that public education loses its best and brightest teachers after less than three years in the profession, while retaining its least capable teachers for the entirety of their careers (Schelechty and Vance, 1981).

During the past two decades, while the litany of depressing statistics about teachers and teacher effectiveness has lengthened, a quiet revolution in research on school learning has been under way. The practical tools and techniques growing out of this rapidly expanding body of knowledge have only begun to be applied to the practice of teaching and to the education of teachers. Recent advances in our understanding of specific factors that directly influence school learning are due at least in part to major shifts in the direction of educational research. Although many of the conceptual models that support new directions in educational research (Barker, 1968; Bloom, 1974; Carroll,

1963; Gagne, 1977; Glaser, 1963; Skinner, 1953) have been under construction for at least twenty-five years, only the past decade has seen the first direct, practical applications in the classroom. Bloom (1980) has suggested that these major changes in approaches to school learning are accounted for by at least three fundamental shifts in educational research: (1) the shift from pre-post study of teacher and student characteristics to the direct observation of the learning environment; (2) the shift from comprehensive theories of learning to models (explanatory structures) that establish direct, causal links between specific events and behaviors and specific learning outcomes; and (3) the shift from an emphasis on *stable* variables to *alterable* variables in education.

It is the third shift that contains perhaps the most exciting and powerful implications for the future of special education and special teachers. To a much greater degree than regular education, the definitions, categories, and classification systems that form the taxonomy of special education are derived from stable variables—IQ, socioeconomic status, a vast array of psychometric indices of aptitude, race, grades, and parent characteristics. These are the types of stable variables used to classify children and to predict their school performance in particular and their personal-social adaptation in general. An unintended result of conceptualizing and organizing education exclusively around stable factors such as these is that too many children are sentenced to a school career of inadequacy, incompetence, negative feelings about self and about learning, impaired productivity, and reduced life chances.

In contrast, an educational discipline that defines itself and its clients in terms of variables presents a far more positive prognosis. For example, redefining aptitude for specific skills (language, computation, and movement) as *learning rate* rather than capacity to learn permits aptitude to be treated as an alterable characteristic (Carroll, 1963). The use of alterable variables to identify and intervene with exceptional children focuses on specific characteristics that have been shown to increase learning performance. At the same time, the use of alterable variables to define teaching provides specific links between teacher behavior, instructional management, and student outcomes.

How will the education of special teachers be influenced during the next decade by the changing picture of teaching and learning that has emerged over the past decade? How can the positive and negative features of the current state of the art of education be realistically linked to the variety of alternative futures that the next decade holds in store? Burdin (1981) has suggested that future studies are too important to be conducted only by a few scholars and professional planners. Teachers, administrators, and teacher educators also have an obligation to become actively involved in the creation of the future of teaching and learning.

The Need to Look Ahead

There is a saying among futurists that the reason they study the future is that the future is where they will spend the rest of their lives. Put another way, we cannot change the past and we can do very little to alter the present, but there is a great deal we can do to change the course of future events. The future is a fresh and new starting place to try to correct past and present inequities, to create new and better systems and structures, and to bring about more desired and desirable states of affairs. The future holds a new series of unoccurred events that are subject, in great measure, to our creative insight and inventive ability. The hope of making a new start by inventing and choosing more preferred alternatives lies in the future.

The establishment of the Congressional Clearinghouse on the Future is one of numerous examples of the impact that futurism has had on our national government. The Clearinghouse publishes a monthly newsletter (*What's Next*), publications (*Public Policy Primers*) on emerging national issues (including names of people around the country involved in researching each issue), and a legislative summary of each issue. The Clearinghouse also maintains a list (*Talent Bank*) of names of the individuals who are involved in some aspect of futures work (for example, trend analysis, civic leadership, and education). TEAM (Trend Evaluation and Monitoring Program) is the first trend-monitoring program ever begun on Capitol Hill. By scanning some seventy national and international publications, over 100 members of Congress and staff personnel track emerging issues in this program of the Congressional Clearinghouse on the Future.

The further influence of long-range thinking, planning, and impact is evidenced by the term *foresight*. One dictionary definition of foresight includes the notion of thoughtful regard or provision for the future or prudent forethought. The concept of foresight has gained circulation among the United States Congress as an expression of concern for the impact of legislation upon our collective future as Americans. As early as the beginning of the 1970s, the principle of foresight was included in the formation of the Congressional Research Service in the Library of Congress. The first full impact forecast (foresight) to become national legislation was contained in a bill introduced by Senator Gary Hart of Colorado (S.B. 1363), which deals with the expansion of electrical production through cogeneration, that is, the multiple use of energy in industrial production.

The recent and continuing series of educational crises cited in the introduction to this chapter are analogous to the economic crises facing this country today. Couldn't our nation have applied the principle of foresight earlier? Can we do it in education? Can we do it now?

A basic assumption of this chapter is that planned change in education is possible. We do not have to and must not continue "business as usual." The future of education is the responsibility of all of us who accept the label of educator, education researcher, teacher, or educational administrator. That we do something about the future of special teacher education is not enough. More importantly, what is done to affect future events should lead us to a future that is an improvement on the past and the present. Future studies is a participatory process that is described as "inventing a desirable future" for special teacher education. Several different approaches to futures invention will be described briefly in this chapter.

Transition from the Present

The focus here is on *group* inventions. We are accustomed to individuals who invent, seek a patent for, and market their products. In the case of the future of special teacher education, many heads are better than one. The first step toward acquiring the tool of futures invention may be the most difficult because it requires us to change the way we think and solve problems. Webster (1977) has compiled a list of changes in emphasis for the year 2000 that will help illustrate this thought transition. These changes are listed in Table 1.

Although none of us is likely to agree entirely with Webster's list, new thinking is possible and often necessary for realizing constructive future change. The Wright Brothers in 1903 were told it couldn't be done—"That much weight cannot be supported in air for a sufficient distance to be practical as a means of any more than folly" (National Park Service, 1977)—by people who could not see beyond here-and-now thinking. Likewise, when Thomas Edison was trying to develop the electric light in 1878, a committee of the British Parliament concluded that Edison's ideas on electric illumination were unworthy of the attention of practical or scientific men (Wall Street Journal, 1967). There are many ways of breaking out of our here-and-now thought processes. In futures invention, it is important to leave one's normal work place, go to a retreat setting, shift gears from involvement with today's problems, and open one's creative and too-seldom-used brain power to frame a valued and desired context for the future of education. This process, or a similar one, can and must occur.

Who Is Looking Ahead: Approaches to Futures Invention

Robert Theobald, a well-known futurist, has made an attempt to classify futurists (Theobald, n.d.). First, there are the *trend extrapolists*. Trend

Table 1. Selected from Webster's "From/To" List on the Future of Education

From Old Emphasis On	To New Emphasis On
Closed systems	Open systems
Authoritarianism	Humanism
The needs of the economy	The needs of the individual and society
Rote learning	Discovery
Kindergarten through 12th grade	Early childhood development and adult continuing education
Poor instructional art	Scientific basis of instruction
Passive learners	Active learners, student-initiated learning
External rewards	Internal rewards
Purely cognitive	Balance between cognitive, affective, and conative
Fragmentation of knowledge	Unity and synthesis of knowledge
Competition	Cooperation
Memorization/regurgitation	Learning to learn
School/state requirements	Self-actualization
Teacher autonomy	Learner autonomy

Source: Webster (1977)

extrapolists do not assume or imagine any fundamental change in our social or governmental structure. There are both positive and negative trend extrapolists. Herman Kahn is an example of the optimistic futurist (postive trend extrapolist) who believes things can and will get better and better. The positive trend extrapolist can be characterized by the statement that "it is possible to provide everyone on earth with a good standard of living within a century." Among the negative trend extrapolists, the pessimistic futurists, there is also the general belief that there will be no fundamental change in the way our society operates. Change, they believe, must occur from the top down. Theobald characterizes negative trend extrapolists with a quotation from Arthur Koestler's *The Call Girls:* "We are a horrible race, living in horrible times. Perhaps we should have the courage to think of horrible remedies." The technocrats in this category are those who feel that the only way to straighten things out is to redesign the society's bureaucracy and put people in boxes whether they like it or not. The technocrats believe that the alternative is complete disaster. Both the positive and negative trend extrapolists believe that the traditional institutional structures that have brought us to our present point of crisis can still serve to pull us out. Their style is—if it doesn't fit, force it!

A second class of futurists are the *romanticists,* typified by Charles Reich, author of *The Greening of America.* The romanticists reflect the ideals of the communes of the 1960s. The philosophy of the romanticists might be—"The world will work most successfully if man is left fully free to define his own role."

Finally, there is Theobald's own view: *systems thinking.* Systems thinkers hold the belief that societies can and must be changed. The change must be toward a more human and humane society, one that values the best qualities of humankind. In order to apply systems thinking, we must take the time to discover the "real" forces that are operating now and influencing human history. We must imagine creatively the future we want, and we must design the necessary methods that will move us from the *present future* (the future that will happen without our intervention) into a future we choose (design or invent).

Who Is Looking Ahead: What Is Recommended

"No generally accepted definition of what comprises the future field currently exists. This is not a serious problem in the formative stages of some purposeful activity; in fact, it may even be of considerable advantage to allow for exploration, experimentation, and trial and error" (Amara, 1980, p. 1). Forecasting and futurism are processes of working with change. When one is examining the details of an event, the greater the disparity between what should be taking place and what is taking place, the greater the incentive for futures planning.

The approach to future studies promulgated in this chapter may be classified as one type of systems thinking called futures invention. Futures invention is based on the following assumptions (Hanberry and others, 1975):

1. The future can be invented.
2. Our images of the future influence our activities in the present.
3. It is not enought to simply think about the future; we must participate in its development.
4. The more alternatives we have for the future, the greater opportunity we have to invent the desired future.
5. People normally use short-range crisis strategies rather than long-range systematic strategies.

6. A planned future has known desirable outcomes with known ways of causing those outcomes to occur.
7. The more you are able to leap into the future and experience some moments in future-time, the greater the chance of making the future come out the way you want it to.

Prior to examining the implications of futures invention for special teacher education, it will be useful to make the distinction between two major types of forecasting. One of the three basic premises that Roy Amara (1980), president of the Institute for the Future and experienced consultant on futures planning, posits is that the future is not predictable. Likewise, James R. Bright (1978), professor of technology management in the Graduate School of Business Administration, University of Texas at Austin, talks about the difficulty of predicting the future by describing a forecast by A. W. Beckerton, a leading Canadian scientist, in 1926. Beckerton spoke about the impossibility of a moon trip: "This foolish idea of shooting at the moon is an example of the absurd length to which vicious specialization will carry scientists working in thought-time compartments" (p. 7).

Although the future of special teacher education may not be predictable, neither is it predetermined; more than one future is possible. Educators can help bring about the more desirable of these alternative futures by deliberate choice and design.

There are two major categories or philosophic bases for forecasts derived from the earlier categories of futurists: extrapolary and normative. Typical of the extrapolary forecasting methods is the extension of trend lines such as population growth curves. Trend line projections are based upon the assumption that events generally advance in a relatively orderly manner over time. Extrapolary forecasting is useful but not sufficient for gaining knowledge about future possibilities. For example, one may predict the world population for the year 2056, but this prediction may be in considerable error due to unknown intervening events such as nuclear war.

Normative forecasting, on the other hand, is goal-oriented, image-driven (Amara, 1980), and prescriptive. Normative forecasting may include extrapolary or exploratory forecasting to examine various alternative futures, but will go farther by arriving at a series of future choices about desirable or preferable alternatives—futures which "ought to be." Futures invention is consonant with the philosophy, aims, and methods of the normative approach to forecasting.

Learning the necessary skills and processes by which desirable futures may be planned is a desirable goal for special teacher education and training. A partial list of these futures skills might include:

- Developing positive communication patterns between individuals and among groups
- The ability to work among and within individuals as well as groups
- Utilizing a cooperative rather than a competitive philosophy in working with persons who have special needs
- Learning how to learn and teaching others to become self-directed learners
- Being a resource person and learning facilitator, rather than just an answer-giver.

Some of the processes that special education teachers may use to invent desired futures will evolve from their special skills but will also come from other professionals (for example, adult educators) who are now creating and testing such processes. One such process has evolved over eight to ten years and began with work designed to combine citizen participation for involvement and change with a sense of the future (Ziegler, 1978). A major underlying purpose in these processes is to give individuals and groups the awareness and the tools to engage in greater self-government, greater self-direction, and to do so with greater consciousness and deliberate choice.

If, as Burdin (1981) suggests, the skills of future studies are indispensable tools for educators, how can they be practically and productively applied to the education of special teachers? The final two sections of the chapter are devoted to an attempt to answer that question.

Special Educators Looking at the Future

This section sets out five major areas of teaching and special teacher education to which the strategy of futures invention can be productively applied: the conceptual base of special education, curricula, teacher preparation, continuing teacher education, and the classroom.

The five broad areas of education are not intended to encompass the whole of teaching and teacher education, nor do they incorporate the social, political, and economic context of education. The purpose here is to illustrate that one or any combination of areas can serve as the medium for planning and evaluation through futures invention.

The Conceptual Base of Special Education. This is the most esoteric and the most practical concern for the future of special education. Is it possible to plan a realistic future for special teacher education that eliminates the distorting, stigmatizing effects of categorical labels and at the same time retains the unique, hard-won, and growing taxonomy of exceptionality? Hobbs's (1975) work on issues surrounding the conceptual base of exceptionality makes an important distinction between *classification* and *labeling*. He argues against labeling children but urges fellow professionals to extend, elaborate, and further articulate the classification system (taxonomy) of special education. Indeed, the hallmark of a mature discipline is a rich, highly specific, empirically established taxonomy. Problems have also arisen because the conceptual structure of special education is comprised of many concepts that are empirically unsound, imprecise, and have much surplus meaning. Abuses occur when broad, general concepts are used to label children mentally retarded, emotionally disturbed, or developmentally disabled. The proper study of exceptionality holds that educators apply objective, accurate information about the conditions that are most pertinent to development and learning (adaptation). The conceptual base becomes distorted when the end result of the process of referral, assessment, and placement is the application of a label rather than the systematic classification of identified barriers to effective adaptation.

A shift in educational research from stable to alterable variables may help to provide the structure and the energy needed to establish a taxonomy that allows, even encourages, classification rather than labeling. By focusing on alterable variables as the basis for classification, special educators could transform the present conceptual base that emphasizes prediction and inference to a concern for process factors that link means and ends in teaching and learning. Bloom (1980) has suggested that if educators believe that little can be done to affect the adaptive behavior of individuals, then their efforts will give high priority to predicting and diagnosing behavior and to categorizing children at an early age. Stable variables such as IQ and aptitude are perfectly suited for such purposes. This approach ensures education that is effective for a few individuals but relegates many students to a mediocre level of performance and some to utter failure.

Futures invention for teaching and preparation of teachers must give careful consideration to the conceptual base of special education. The alternative futures of special education will ultimately depend on the conceptual framework of the discipline. Will that framework rest on stable or alterable variables?

Curricula. The content of education and the manner of organizing that content is the essence of school curricula. Curricula, like the constitution, will and should continue to spawn debate along the continuum of strict and liberal construction. Any reasonable examination of alternative futures of special education and the preparation of professional special educators must include curricula as a high priority. There are at least three aspects of curricula that can serve as important vehicles for futures invention—policy, content, and structure.

Who should establish the policies that govern school curricula—the federal government, state boards of education, professional education organizations, teacher unions, or university curricula specialists? To what extent, if any, should schools reflect a nationally uniform curriculum? How can curricula policy most effectively and equitably account for the special education requirements of exceptional students? Should curricula content continue to be circumscribed by the education of students from kindergarten through grade twelve? What obligations does public education have for curricula related to career cycles and to lifelong learning? How can the content of school curricula best accommodate the rapid growth in knowledge and technological developments that are likely to continue at an increasingly faster pace?

The structure of a school curriculum in large measure dictates how and by whom the content of the curriculum will be delivered. An important implication for the future of special education is how schools should be organized to most effectively, efficiently, and ethically serve the educational needs of exceptional individuals. In that connection, the roles of special teachers and the expansion of numbers and types of subprofessionals and paraprofessionals seem likely to continue the metamorphosis that began with the training of the first special educator.

Well-planned and appropriate use of futures invention by caring professionals and lay citizens can provide alternative futures for special education curricula policy and content that are negotiated rather than imposed or established by default. Educators can help shape the future of school curricula by actively involving themselves in the creation of the future. Examining the ideal future in the light of present realities requires asking the right questions as well as seeking answers and solutions.

Teacher Preparation. The education of special teachers is closely tied to the larger institution of teacher education. Teacher education has been sharply criticized for its slow adaptation to social and technological forces and advances in research knowledge about learning, development, and instruction. Special teacher education is a relatively recent entrant into the profession and for that reason alone may not have yet become as conservative as teacher education in general. In addition to being a more youthful discipline, special teacher education has had to establish itself as a legitimate member of the profession with a unique role to play. These conditions have encouraged the first twenty-five years of special teacher education to be proactive in nature. The quality of special teachers and their record of performance is generally well regarded, especially since about 1970. Now that special education is an established discipline and the role of the special educator is recognized within the education profession, the necessity for looking ahead is paramount.

Representatives of the key social institutions in teacher education—schools of education, teachers' colleges, and state departments of education—

can employ futures invention as a method of planning alternative approaches to the future of teacher education. The most fundamental questions and issues must be considered. For example, should institutions of higher education continue to be unilaterally responsible for teacher education? Should teacher education and professional licensing be taken over by teachers through their associations and unions? Should the preparation of teachers be turned over to liberal arts scholars or to state departments of education? If colleges and universities are to continue as the primary training sites, how can quality assurance be accomplished?

Even if the key social institutions in teacher education cannot or will not soften their current defensive and reactionary posture, those institutional components charged with policy making and management of special teacher education should assertively engage in planning the future. The ideal approach to futures planning would integrate teacher educators, educational researchers, state department of public instruction leaders, local education agency personnel, teacher association representatives, legislators, and lay leaders. No matter related to the education and certification of special teachers should be off-limits to the evaluation and planning process. Effective teacher education can result only when those responsible have the foresight and courage to question the holiest assumptions and practices of the profession and have the confidence to be accountable.

Continuing Teacher Education. Properly planned, the future of special teacher education would include continuing education as well as preservice education. Continuing teacher education (inservice education) is set apart from teacher education in the present discussion because the two components are separate entities in current practice.

Responsibility for what sometimes masquerades as continuing teacher education has been assumed largely by local schools. In fact, only rarely are there efforts to provide a systematic continuing education program for teachers during their professional service. Corrigan's (1978) analysis of the status of inservice education points out that few school districts spend even as much as 1 percent of their budgets on continuing education. In contrast, some corporations put as much as 10 percent of their gross income into inservice education for personnel. Other professions (such as medicine, law, and accounting) give high priority to the continuing education of practitioners. Still another indication of the low priority given to continuing teacher education is the near total lack of research evidence concerning the efficacy of various approaches to inservice education.

Futures planning needs to consider alternative strategies for systematically linking preservice and inservice education. Such efforts must integrate (or, at least, coordinate) the various institutions and agencies involved. The continued absence of institution-level consideration of the future of continuing teacher education does not preclude action by special educators.

There are many basic questions to be answered. For example, by whom and how should policies governing inservice education be established? To what extent should the teaching profession be responsible for its own continuing education? Should inservice education be restricted to teachers, that is, what is the obligation of teacher educators, principals, secretaries, aides, and others for continuing education? How can the unique strengths and resources of a school be most effectively incorporated into a program of inservice education? What are some realistic strategies for integrating university-based teacher educators and preservice teachers with local education agencies, teachers, and administrators? How can continuing teacher education be appropriately valued and rewarded by the power structure of the school system? Should continuing education include emotional and personal-social development (mental health) of teachers? How can inservice education most effectively fill the professional and personal growth needs of *individual* teachers? Should the certification of teachers be linked to the outcomes of continuing teacher education over the first years of the teaching career?

The Classroom. It is the classroom that serves as the crucible for all the elements that make up the teaching-learning process. Classroom is used here to refer to the learning site, whether it be a regular classroom, resource room, developmental daycare program, or nursery. The learner outcomes, measured and unmeasured, short-term and long-term, become primary evidence for the efficacy of teacher education. The classroom is the stage where teachers come face to face with learners in a context comprised of the material and conditions of learning. Incredibly, it is only within the past decade that educators have begun to systematically examine the relationship between specific teacher behaviors and pupil outcomes. After a half century of pre- and post-testing, then studying results in order to infer (guess) what went on in the classroom to produce those results, educators have finally come into the classroom to study the teaching-learning process directly. Despite the recency of this fundamental shift in focus, classroom research has already discovered links between teacher behavior and pupil outcomes that had been previously studied by indirect methods. It is not yet unequivocally clear if these same relationships occur with special teachers and exceptional students.

Beginning with the Coleman Report (1966), a succession of major studies on the effects of schooling in America sent an important message— schools don't make a difference. Restated, that message was teachers don't make a difference. One of the most important implications of classroom research findings requires a slight, but important, change in that message—teachers *can* make a difference. If classroom research continues to confirm and sustain present findings and trends, the future of teaching and teacher education can be bright and positive, even exciting. Once again, the point of this chapter is to show that teacher educators and teachers must participate in the invention of the future. Participation requires the willingness to invest in the future of special teacher education but it also requires the acquisition of the skills that constitute the futures invention process.

Futures Invention and Skills Procedures

Since the 1960s there have been a growing number of futurists who have been experimenting with practical applications of the normative forecasting approach to the future. One group comes from a formal background in education and many others with a subspecialty in the education of adult learners. Applying normative forecasting and simultaneously utilizing the small-group methods of the adult educator has produced a number of paradigms or models for inventing the future. Among the most promising developments, two emerge as subjects for illustration. Although it must be recognized that futures studies and the attempts to apply its theories (futures invention) are still in their infancy, the major elements of two philosophically similar systems will be described for purposes of illustration. In the following description, the reader will be able to visualize the key elements included in a futures invention program design. (The terms *futures invention* and *planning* are used synonymously in this section.)

Setting. One major reason for the importance of the setting is to allow participants to make a transition from everyday present to the future. A neutral, non-workplace location should be selected. The setting should be free of outside distractions, including avoidable telephone calls and other back-at-the-office contact. The location should have multiple spaces for various sizes of groups, including general large-group meetings and separate small-group sessions.

Participants. A number of participant characteristics will depend upon the specific futures invention project (for example, type of institution, size of work group, administrative structure, and overall planning objectives). Other important factors are:

1. All participants should have a vested interest in planning outcomes.
2. All planning constraints, necessary parameters to limit action, and other "givens" should be clearly stated at the outset.
3. If the field for planning represents a very large number of persons, then the futures invention group selected should represent a cross-section of the larger population.
4. All participants should engage in the project on a voluntary basis.

5. Some explicit commitment to the overall goals should be obtained prior to workshop participation to ensure an honest participant investment.
6. All participants should become actively involved in the process and be directly invested in planning outcomes by their participation.
7. The process (workshop, retreat, or planning activity) should have the full support and representative participation of senior-level administration.

Time Frame. A creative and meaningful futures invention cannot be completed in one day. Most futures invention processes have a preplanning phase, giving participants a base for participation; a workshop phase, at least three days in length; and a postmeeting phase for final decisions and implementation. The three-day workshop phase should be conducted without outside interruption.

Staff. It is imperative that workshop facilities and leaders have some training in adult education methods and in futures invention theory. Since it is unclear just what training constitutes a facilitator in adult education and even less clear for a facilitator in futures invention, these persons should have the following experience and commitments:

1. Training in group process, adult learning theory, and experience in administering workshops utilizing experiential learning exercises.
2. A general familiarity with the literature in futures studies and some training in futures invention or parallel processes.
3. A commitment to the project and previous experience in using futures planning for themselves.
4. The ability to include participant representatives in preworkshop planning, workshop design, and designing postworkshop experiences.
5. Training and/or experience in using positive strategies to deal with and resolve intragroup conflict. (Conflict is a natural and desirable aspect of futures planning but it must be well channeled by the group and by group facilitators.)

Workshop Phase. The preliminary design of the workshop is one of the most critical. In this phase it is important to:

1. Design the workshop to meet the overall planning goals.
2. Have participants well prepared for their participation in advance of the workshop.
3. Design preworkshop materials to lead directly into the workshop philosophy (futures invention), goals (established by the planning organization), and the process itself (as designed by facilitators and client group representatives).

4. Secure a final commitment from each participant after all aspects of the planning experience have been made clear.

At the outset of the workshop it may be necessary to have a series of get-acquainted exercises or group experiences. During this early period, broad workshop goals are being interpreted into more personal goals by the individual participants.

The goals are long-term and personal at first but become more other-oriented during the workshop. There must be a direct relationship between the broad planning goals and the outcomes but these may be supplemented or *surpassed* by the participants' creative imagination. Personal goals are *events* that have not yet occurred and are therefore handled by each participant's imagination. Often participants are able to construct more specific goals that are innovative and/or inventive — surpassing expectations. It is important that participants understand that all workshop goals must be possible to attain and eventually implement once they are properly refined.

During key points in the workshop, clarification sessions become very helpful to participants and to task groups. Finishing a sentence with "What I mean by this goal is . . . ." will help everyone become clearer and gradually more specific about the desired workshop outcomes. Stating these final outcomes clearly and specifically provides the definition for deciding when the not-yet-occurred event has been achieved. That is, the clear specification statements allow one to recognize these future events as they arrive.

It was mentioned earlier in this chapter that determining the impact of the forecast (as with the foresight consideration in Congressional legislation) will aid in determining the secondary and tertiary implications of intended actions. Foresight and impact consideration will also expose implicit value assumptions for review. As these actions and implications are determined, building a complete picture of the future (a scenario) will draw out the action decisions to logical conclusions for final review in the planning mode.

After individual participants have created and announced to the group their own ideal future events, these individuals will come together into common task forces willing to work toward goals with similar outcomes and values. This begins the realization that the future, like the present, is a shared experience and that an ideal way to design that desired future is by the active participation of those who share the responsibility for its design. Task forces are formed by individuals whose future scenarios have some or all of the following:

- Common philosophy
- Similar value systems
- Compatible goals or objectives
- Shared perspectives on goal attainment (methods)
- Agreement on outcomes.

Teams (task forces) now begin building a community scenario that, to the greatest degree possible, includes the essentials of each individual scenario.

In the process of future scenario implementation, the larger group may opt for one or more of a wide range of strategies. It may be helpful for group facilitators to assist the group with exercises and group experiences for the purpose of selecting the implementation strategies. Often a master road map leading back from the desired future goal to the present can be systematically constructed.

Sometimes two or three task forces will agree to work together. This kind of team building may go on successively at different levels until, finally, one master scenario is acceptable to the entire group as their desired future, in keeping with the goals agreed to at the outset.

Postworkshop Events. Following the formal process, the workshop facilitators and participant representatives will have a series of meetings for the purpose of designing implementation strategies based upon the master planning scenario. Policy teams might now be asked to deal with specific internal administrative or organizational changes or with external matters such as establishing contacts with regulatory agencies, political bodies, and local special interest groups.

Summary and Conclusions

Cries for the reform of education are justified due to the pressing learning needs of society. These learning needs, according to many futurists, have been created from the increasing pace of social change and social transformation. The transformation, according to one widely published futurist (Theobald, 1976), is from the end of the industrial era (fueled by the industrial revolution) and the coming of the communications era (characterized by change, complexity, and the need for cooperation rather than competition). Each of us with sensitivity to these complex changes in our society feels the need for more knowledge, skill in coping with change, help in acquiring vocational abilities for our present or a new career, and reassurance that we the people are in fact in control of our future.

When the needs of society change and we gain new insights into the process of teaching and learning, it becomes necessary to alter our teaching/learning institutions. One of these teaching/learning institutions is the university and its school of education. When schools of education face changing learning needs, gain new insights into how persons learn, and are called upon to train leaders for very different tasks, the faculties of these schools of education must themselves learn and change to meet the new needs.

Futures invention is an emerging process that itself is representative of transformation. Futures invention and other processes can help us to cope with change, implement new knowledge, engage in group planning, evaluate where we are going, and how we will get there. Futurists have emerged because of the need to cope with change and our present social transformation. Basically, the futurist perspective gives us (as educators) a tool for dealing with change in education. There are many systems that might be utilized to bring about change. What is important is that we control change in positive and useful ways so that it does not control us, causing our responses to become only reactive, piecemeal, and confused.

Inventing our future is a way to keep our priorities clear by asking where we want to go, what are the essential value implications, which needs and competencies are most important, what administrative structure should be utilized, and so on. Inventing our future is one way to keep our collective minds focused on the appropriate needs of our special learners and to use our energies to educate and train new leaders for this purpose.

References

Amara, R. *The Futures Field.* Menlo Park, Calif.: Institute for the Future, 1980.
Barker, R. G. *Ecological Psychology: Concepts and Methods for Studying the Environment of Human Behavior.* Stanford, Calif.: Stanford University Press, 1968.
Bloom, B. S. "Time and Learning." *American Psychologist,* 1974, *29,* 682–688.
Bloom, B. S. "The New Direction in Educational Research: Alterable Variables." *Phi Delta Kappan,* February 1980, 382–385.
Bright, J. R. *A Brief Introduction to Technology Forecasting Concepts and Exercises.* Austin: University of Texas, Graduate School of Business Administration, 1978.
Burdin, J. L. "Alternative Futurism: An Indispensable Tool for Educators." *World Future Society Bulletin,* January/February 1981, 16–22.
Carroll, J. B. "A Model of School Learning." *Teacher's College Record,* 1963, *64,* 723–733.
Coleman, J. S. *Equality of Educational Opportunity.* Washington, D.C.: U.S. Department of Health, Education, and Welfare, Office of Education, 1966.
Corrigan, D. "The Present State of Teacher Education and Needed Reforms." In M. C. Reynolds (Ed.), *Futures of Exceptional Students: Emerging Structures.* Washington, D.C.: U.S. Office of Education, Bureau for Education of the Handicapped, National Support Systems Project, 1978.
Gagne, R. *The Conditions of Learning.* (3rd ed.) New York: Holt, Rinehart and Winston, 1977.
Gallagher, J. J. "Future of Special Education." In J. Paul (Ed.), *Understanding and Working with Parents of Children with Special Needs.* New York: Holt, Rinehart and Winston, 1981.
Glaser, R. "Instructional Technology and the Measurement of Learning Outcomes." *American Psychologist,* 1963, *18,* 519–521.
Hanberry, G. C., and others. *Inventing the Future: Participatory Planning Process for Alternative Futures.* College Park: University of Maryland, Conferences and Institutes Division, 1975.
Hobbs, N. (Ed.). *The Futures of Children: Recommendations of the Project on Classification of Exceptional Children.* San Francisco: Jossey-Bass, 1975.

National Park Service. *Wright Brothers.* Washington, D.C.: U.S. Department of the Interior, 1977.

Public Policy Primers. Washington, D.C.: Congressional Clearinghouse on the Future, 1980.

Reich, C. A. *The Greening of America: How the Youth Revolution is Trying to Make America Livable.* New York: Random House, 1970.

Schelechty, P., and Vance, V. "Do Academically Able Teachers Leave Education? The North Carolina Case." *Phi Delta Kappan,* October 1981, 106–112.

Skinner, B. F. *Science and Human Behavior.* New York: Macmillan, 1953.

Talent Bank. Washington, D.C.: Congressional Clearinghouse on the Future, 1980.

Theobald, R. *Beyond Despair, Directions for America's Third Century.* Washington, D.C.: New Republic Books, 1976.

Theobald, R. "The Second Copernican Revolution." Unpublished manuscript, n.d.

Wall Street Journal. *Here Comes Tomorrow: Living and Working in the Year 2000.* Princeton, N.J.: Dow Jones Books, 1967.

Webster, R. E. "Project on Human Potential and the Year 2000." In P. Dickson (Ed.), *The Future File.* Austin, Tex.: Learning Concepts, 1977.

What's Next. Washington, D.C.: Congressional Clearinghouse on the Future, 1980.

Wirtz, W., and others. *On Further Examination: Report of the Advisory Panel on the Scholastic Aptitude Test Score Decline.* New York: College Entrance Examination Board, 1977.

Ziegler, W. L. "Futures-Invention: A New Tool for Formulating Population Policy." In E. Glassheim, C. Cargille, and C. Hoffman (Eds.), *Key Issues in Population Policy: Capon Springs Public Policy Conference No. 1.* Washington, D.C.: University Press of America, 1978.

Paul F. Fendt is associate director of extension and continuing education and a clinical assistant professor of education in the School of Education, University of North Carolina at Chapel Hill.

Marvin D. Wyne is associate professor of education in the School of Education at the University of North Carolina at Chapel Hill.

Index

A

Access, equity of, and manpower planning, 47-48
Accreditation, and program quality, 4
Administration, of field-based programs, 55-59
Admissions, for field-based programs, 60-62
Alexander, C., 75, 83
Alexander, W. M., 36
Amara, R., 93, 94, 104
Arends, J. H., 27, 28, 35
Arends, R. I., 27, 28, 35
Attitudes: analysis of, 73-85; correlates of, 78-79; modification of, 79-83

B

Bailey, D. B., Jr., 51-71
Baird, L., 17
Bandura, A., 74, 83
Barker, R. G., 88, 104
Bates, P., 26, 37
Baucom, L. D., 3-18
Beckerton, A. W., 94
Behrens, T., 23, 25, 27, 35
Black, T., 15, 17
Blanton, L. P., 39-50
Bloom, B. S., 88, 89, 96, 104
Boote, K., 77, 83
Braun, B. L., 78, 84
Bright, J. R., 94, 104
Buchanan, M. L., 22, 29, 35
Bullock, L. M., 82, 83
Burdin, J. L., 22, 35, 89, 95, 104
Bureau of Education for the Handicapped, 23; Division of Personnel Preparation of, 41; Project of Cooperative Manpower Planning in Special Education of, 40-41. *See also* Office of Special Education
Burke, W. I., 19-37, 79, 83
Burton, T., 76, 84
Buttery, T. J., 77, 78, 83

C

Carey, J. A., 79, 83
Carroll, J. B., 88-89, 104
Cartwright, C. A., 79, 81-82, 84
Clark, M. J., 9, 11, 12, 17
Classification, labeling distinct from, 96
Classroom, and futures invention, 99-100
Cline, R., 78, 83
Coleman, J. S., 99, 104
Conant, J. B., 20, 26, 35
Congressional Clearinghouse on the Future, 90
Consortium. *See* Planning consortium
Continuing education, and futures invention, 98-99
Corrigan, D. C., 25, 26, 28, 35, 36, 98, 104
Cremin, L. A., 32-33, 34, 35
Crossland, C. L., 39-50
Curriculum: change legitimizing for, 26-29; competency-based, 26; concepts, assumptions, and questions about, 19-22; conditions necessitating change in, 22-30; content appropriate for, 25-26; content revision of, 24-25; defined, 19-20; design of, 32-34; evaluation of, 29-30, 34-35; and federal assistance, 23; and futures invention, 96-97; and governance, 27-28, 30-32; model of, 30-35; process for change in, 19-37; reform in, components of, 23-24; sources of, 20-22
Czatlocky, K., 76-77, 84

D

Dean's Grant projects, 2, 23, 27, 29-30
DeLeo, A. V., 79, 83
Delivery, of field-based programs, 63-67
Denmark, G., 26, 35, 36
Drew, C. J., 22, 27, 28, 29, 35-36
Duncan, J. R., 41, 50

107

E

Edison, T., 91
Education for all Handicapped Children Act of 1975 (P.L. 94-142), 1; and cooperative planning, 41, 42; and curricular change, 21, 22-23, 25, 26, 30, 31; and mainstreaming, 73, 75
Educational research, shifts in, 89
Educational Testing Service, 10
Edwards, R., 76, 83
Elizabeth City Graduate Center, field-based program at, 55
Elizabeth City State University, 55
Eurich, A. C., 19, 36
Evaluation: of curriculum, 29-30, 34-35; of doctoral programs, 9-14; features of, 7-8; of field-based programs, 67-71; instrument for, 10-12; of program impact, 68-69; of quality, 70; of staff satisfaction, 69-70; of teacher education programs, 3-18; of undergraduate and master's programs, 5-9
Ezzell, C., 61, 71

F

Faculty: and change, 27; characteristics of, 10, 11; and field-based programs, 62-63; as governance unit, 31; motivations of, 63
Fayetteville Graduate Center, field-based program at, 54, 62, 68, 69-70
Fayetteville State University, 54
Federal government: and curriculum change, 23; and planning cooperation, 40-42
Fendt, P. F., 87-105
Field-based programs: administration of, 55-59; admissions for, 60-62; analysis of, 51-71; concept of, 52; content of, 64-65; cooperation in, 55-56; course packaging for, 67; development conditions for, 56-57; evaluation of, 67-71; faculty and, 62-63; funding and development of, 57-58; increase of, 52-53; issues in, 55-71; mutual benefits in, 55; planning investment for, 58-59; practica in, 65-67; program delivery issues of, 63-67; students in, 59-60

Fine, M. J., 77, 78, 84
Fishbein, J. E., 73n
Fishell, K. N., 27, 36
Fisher, E. B., 80-81, 82, 83
Foresight, concept of, 90
Fox, W. L., 27, 36
Frith, G. H., 76, 83
Futures invention: analysis of, 87-105; approaches to, 91-93; areas of, in teacher education, 95-100; as group inventions, 91-92; participants in, 100-101; recommendation for, 93-95; setting for, 100; and skills procedures, 100-103; staff for, 101; time frame for, 101; workshop for, 101-103
Futurism: classification in, 91-93, 94; need for, 87, 90-91

G

Gagne, R., 89, 104
Gallagher, J. J., 12, 17, 87, 104
George, A., 36
Gilberts, R. S., 28, 36
Glaser, R., 89, 104
Glass, R. M., 80, 84
Governance: and curriculum change, 27-28, 30-32; defined, 30-31
Graduate Record Examination (GRE), 60-61
Grosenick, J. K., 23, 27, 35
Grotelueschen, T. S., 26, 29, 36
Guerin, G. R., 76-77, 78, 84

H

Hall, G. E., 27, 29, 36
Hanberry, G. C., 93-94, 104
Haring, N. G., 80, 84
Hart, G., 90
Hartnett, R., 17
Hirshoren, A., 76, 84
Hirst, P. H., 20, 36
Hobbs, N., 95-96, 104
Howsam, R. B., 23, 26, 36

I

Iano, R. P., 84
Imig, D. G., 27-28, 30-31, 36
Iriarte, A. U., 26, 36

Index

A

Access, equity of, and manpower planning, 47-48
Accreditation, and program quality, 4
Administration, of field-based programs, 55-59
Admissions, for field-based programs, 60-62
Alexander, C., 75, 83
Alexander, W. M., 36
Amara, R., 93, 94, 104
Arends, J. H., 27, 28, 35
Arends, R. I., 27, 28, 35
Attitudes: analysis of, 73-85; correlates of, 78-79; modification of, 79-83

B

Bailey, D. B., Jr., 51-71
Baird, L., 17
Bandura, A., 74, 83
Barker, R. G., 88, 104
Bates, P., 26, 37
Baucom, L. D., 3-18
Beckerton, A. W., 94
Behrens, T., 23, 25, 27, 35
Black, T., 15, 17
Blanton, L. P., 39-50
Bloom, B. S., 88, 89, 96, 104
Boote, K., 77, 83
Braun, B. L., 78, 84
Bright, J. R., 94, 104
Buchanan, M. L., 22, 29, 35
Bullock, L. M., 82, 83
Burdin, J. L., 22, 35, 89, 95, 104
Bureau of Education for the Handicapped, 23; Division of Personnel Preparation of, 41; Project of Cooperative Manpower Planning in Special Education of, 40-41. *See also* Office of Special Education
Burke, W. I., 19-37, 79, 83
Burton, T., 76, 84
Buttery, T. J., 77, 78, 83

C

Carey, J. A., 79, 83
Carroll, J. B., 88-89, 104
Cartwright, C. A., 79, 81-82, 84
Clark, M. J., 9, 11, 12, 17
Classification, labeling distinct from, 96
Classroom, and futures invention, 99-100
Cline, R., 78, 83
Coleman, J. S., 99, 104
Conant, J. B., 20, 26, 35
Congressional Clearinghouse on the Future, 90
Consortium. *See* Planning consortium
Continuing education, and futures invention, 98-99
Corrigan, D. C., 25, 26, 28, 35, 36, 98, 104
Cremin, L. A., 32-33, 34, 35
Crossland, C. L., 39-50
Curriculum: change legitimizing for, 26-29; competency-based, 26; concepts, assumptions, and questions about, 19-22; conditions necessitating change in, 22-30; content appropriate for, 25-26; content revision of, 24-25; defined, 19-20; design of, 32-34; evaluation of, 29-30, 34-35; and federal assistance, 23; and futures invention, 96-97; and governance, 27-28, 30-32; model of, 30-35; process for change in, 19-37; reform in, components of, 23-24; sources of, 20-22
Czatlocky, K., 76-77, 84

D

Dean's Grant projects, 2, 23, 27, 29-30
DeLeo, A. V., 79, 83
Delivery, of field-based programs, 63-67
Denmark, G., 26, 35, 36
Drew, C. J., 22, 27, 28, 29, 35-36
Duncan, J. R., 41, 50

107

E

Edison, T., 91
Education for all Handicapped Children Act of 1975 (P.L. 94-142), 1; and cooperative planning, 41, 42; and curricular change, 21, 22-23, 25, 26, 30, 31; and mainstreaming, 73, 75
Educational research, shifts in, 89
Educational Testing Service, 10
Edwards, R., 76, 83
Elizabeth City Graduate Center, field-based program at, 55
Elizabeth City State University, 55
Eurich, A. C., 19, 36
Evaluation: of curriculum, 29-30, 34-35; of doctoral programs, 9-14; features of, 7-8; of field-based programs, 67-71; instrument for, 10-12; of program impact, 68-69; of quality, 70; of staff satisfaction, 69-70; of teacher education programs, 3-18; of undergraduate and master's programs, 5-9
Ezzell, C., 61, 71

F

Faculty: and change, 27; characteristics of, 10, 11; and field-based programs, 62-63; as governance unit, 31; motivations of, 63
Fayetteville Graduate Center, field-based program at, 54, 62, 68, 69-70
Fayetteville State University, 54
Federal government: and curriculum change, 23; and planning cooperation, 40-42
Fendt, P. F., 87-105
Field-based programs: administration of, 55-59; admissions for, 60-62; analysis of, 51-71; concept of, 52; content of, 64-65; cooperation in, 55-56; course packaging for, 67; development conditions for, 56-57; evaluation of, 67-71; faculty and, 62-63; funding and development of, 57-58; increase of, 52-53; issues in, 55-71; mutual benefits in, 55; planning investment for, 58-59; practica in, 65-67; program delivery issues of, 63-67; students in, 59-60

Fine, M. J., 77, 78, 84
Fishbein, J. E., 73n
Fishell, K. N., 27, 36
Fisher, E. B., 80-81, 82, 83
Foresight, concept of, 90
Fox, W. L., 27, 36
Frith, G. H., 76, 83
Futures invention: analysis of, 87-105; approaches to, 91-93; areas of, in teacher education, 95-100; as group inventions, 91-92; participants in, 100-101; recommendation for, 93-95; setting for, 100; and skills procedures, 100-103; staff for, 101; time frame for, 101; workshop for, 101-103
Futurism: classification in, 91-93, 94; need for, 87, 90-91

G

Gagne, R., 89, 104
Gallagher, J. J., 12, 17, 87, 104
George, A., 36
Gilberts, R. S., 28, 36
Glaser, R., 89, 104
Glass, R. M., 80, 84
Governance: and curriculum change, 27-28, 30-32; defined, 30-31
Graduate Record Examination (GRE), 60-61
Grosenick, J. K., 23, 27, 35
Grotelueschen, T. S., 26, 29, 36
Guerin, G. R., 76-77, 78, 84

H

Hall, G. E., 27, 29, 36
Hanberry, G. C., 93-94, 104
Haring, N. G., 80, 84
Hart, G., 90
Hartnett, R., 17
Hirshoren, A., 76, 84
Hirst, P. H., 20, 36
Hobbs, N., 95-96, 104
Howsam, R. B., 23, 26, 36

I

Iano, R. P., 84
Imig, D. G., 27-28, 30-31, 36
Iriarte, A. U., 26, 36

J

Johnson, A. B., 79, 81–82, 84
Jones, L. V., 61, 71

K

Kahn, H., 92
Kirk, S., 12, 17
Kirst, N., 75–76, 84
Knowledge development, and field-based programs, 52
Koestler, A., 92–93

L

Labeling, classification distinct from, 96
Lahti, L. I., 26, 29, 36
Lanzillotti, K., 22, 35
Lawrence, J., 36
Lewis, A. J., 36
Lillie, D. L., 15, 17, 51–71
Loucks, S., 36
Lucas, C. J., 25, 26, 27, 28, 36

M

McFadden, M., 84
McGettigan, J. F., 84
McGough, R. L., 41, 50
Mackie, K., 82, 84
Mainstreaming, and teacher attitudes, 73–85. *See also* Education for All Handicapped Children Act of 1975
Martin, E., 24, 36
Massachusetts, teacher attitudes in, 76
Meckler, R. S., 80, 84
Meyer, E. L., 24, 36
Miller, S. R., 54, 71
Miller, T. L., 71
Moore, J., 77, 78, 84
Morsink, C. V., 35
Murdoch Center, field-based program at, 54

N

Nash, G. L., 77, 78, 84
Nash, R. J., 36
National Council for Accreditation of Teacher Education, 4
National Council of Mathematics Teachers, 21
National Education Association: Committee of Ten of, 22; Committee on the Reorganization of the Secondary Schools, 22
National Park Service, 91, 105
Nelson, M. C., 71
North Carolina: Board of Education in, 46; certification in, 46, 64, 66; Comprehensive System for Personnel Development (CSPD) in, 44; Cooperative Planning Consortium of Special Education Training Programs in, 39–50; Department of Correction in, 44; Legislative Study Commission on Children with Special Needs in, 42; National Teacher Examination in, 88
North Carolina, University of, 18; and field-based programs, 54, 55; and planning consortium, 42–44, 47; Teacher Education Review Program (TERP) at, 5–9; teacher preparation at, 1–2; technical assistance from, 14–17
North Carolina, University of, at Chapel Hill, field-based program of, 51, 53–71
North Carolina Association for Educators, 43
North Carolina Community College System, 43
North Carolina Teacher Observation Scale, 68–69
Northern Illinois University, and field-based education, 54

O

Office of Special Education, 23, 53. *See also* Bureau of Education for the Handicapped

P

Parents and Professionals for Handicapped Children, 43–44
Paul, J. L., 51–71
Perry, M. L., 27, 28, 36
Peters, R. S., 78–79, 84
P. L. 94-142. *See* Education for All Handicapped Children Act of 1975

Planning consortium: analysis of, 39–50; background of, 40–42; genesis of, 42–45; principles of, 48–49; quality and access issues in, 45–48
Practica, in field-based programs, 65–67
Pratt, S. E., 77, 78, 84
Proctor, D. I., 78, 79, 84
Program approval, and quality, 4
Program delivery, field-based, 63–67

Q

Quality: evaluation of, 70; and manpower planning, 45–47
Quality Assurance Program, 15, 17

R

Rader, B. T., 26, 36
Reich, C. A., 93, 105
Resources, characteristics of, 10–11, 12
Reynolds, M. C., 1–2, 26, 27, 36
Riggen, T. F., 80, 82, 84
Rogers, E., 15, 18
Rugg, H., 33, 36
Russell, J. E., 32–33
Ryan, K., 24, 25, 28, 36

S

Saylor, J. G., 19–20, 36
S. B. 1363, 90
Schelechty, P., 88, 105
Schmid, R., 36
Schofer, R. C., 41, 50
Scholastic Aptitude Test, 88
Scriven, M., 24, 29, 36
Sharp, B., 36
Shaw, H., 73n
Shotel, J. R., 81, 82, 84
Simeonsson, R. J., 73–85
Singleton, K., 81, 82, 84
Skinner, B. F., 89, 105
Smith, B. O., 25, 26, 28, 37
Smith, R. R., 3–18
Special education: conceptual base of, 95–96; groups with roles in, 40; legislative mandate for trained personnel in, 39–40; manpower planning consortium for, 39–50; sociopolitical context of, and field-based programs, 53; stable or alterable variables in, 89, 96
State Department of Human Resources (North Carolina), 45; Office for Children of, 43
State Department of Public Instruction (North Carolina), 45, 46, 54; Division for Exceptional Children of, 43
Stedman, D. J., 3–18, 26, 37
Stevens, T. M., 78, 84
Stonebrenner, R. L., 71
Strain, P. S. 75, 83
Strickland, B., 19–37, 79, 83
Students: characteristics of, 10, 11; in field-based programs, 59–60
Surez, A. C., 84

T

Teacher education: assessment of, 3–18; barriers to improvement of, 8; characteristics of, 9; curricular change in, 19–37; defined, 31; doctoral, evaluating, 9–14; field-based programs in, 51–71; and futures invention, 87–105; futures skills in, 94–95; governance of, 27–28, 30–32; growth of programs in, 3–4; master's level, evaluating, 5–9; need for, 1; quality and access issues of, 45–48; state of the art in, 88–89; strength, productivity, and need characteristics of, 6–7; undergraduate, evaluating, 5–9
Teachers: attitudes of, 73–85; interrelated with children, 74–75; number and stability of, 53; strengthening competencies of, 14–17
Technical assistance (TA), process and features of, 14–17
Theobald, R., 91–93, 103, 105
Thomas, C. C., 35
Trend Evaluation and Monitoring Program (TEAM), 90
Trohanis, P. O., 15, 18
Turnbull, A. P., 24, 37

U

U.S. Department of Education, 2
U.S. Office of Education, Elementary Education Model of, 21

V

Vacc, N., 75-76, 84
Vance, V., 88, 105
Variables, stable or alterable, 89, 96

W

Wall Street Journal, 91, 105
Wasik, B. H., 73-85
Webster, R. E., 91, 92, 105

Wechsler, H., 76, 78, 84
Weisenstein, G. R., 28, 36
West, T. L., 26, 37
Whelan, R. J., 82, 83
Williams, H., 84
Wirtz, W., 88, 105
Wright Brothers, 81
Wyne, M. D., 87-105

Z

Ziegler, W. L., 95, 105

DATE DUE			
MAR 10 '84			
APR 18 1987			

LC 3969 .P75 1981   54832

Professional preparation for
teachers of exceptional

Library
St. Joseph's College
Patchogue, N.Y. 11772

Do Not Remove 8/08 Date